Justin Langer
1970 and was ec
ern Australia.
Western Australia in November 1991 against Victoria, while his Test debut for Australia came the following season against the West Indies. By the end of 1999 he had played twenty-seven times for his country, scoring five centuries. He has toured England three times, including with the 1997 Ashes party, and played English league cricket for three seasons before joining Middlesex as their overseas player in 1998. He was appointed captain of Middlesex for the 2000 season.

He is married to Sue, and they have two young children, Jessica and Ali-Rose. He has worked as a stockbroker and now writes a very popular Internet diary.

From Outback to Outfield

A Diary of an English Summer

Justin Langer

HEADLINE

First published in 1999
by HEADLINE BOOK PUBLISHING

First published in paperback in 2000
by HEADLINE BOOK PUBLISHING

10 9 8 7 6 5 4 3 2 1

ISBN 0 7472 6254 3

Typeset by Palimpsest Book Production Limited,
Polmont, Stirlingshire

Printed and bound by
Mackays of Chatham plc, Chatham, Kent

HEADLINE BOOK PUBLISHING
A division of the Hodder Headline Group
338 Euston Road
London NW1 3BH

www.headline.co.uk
www.hodderheadline.com

Contents

INTRODUCTION

It seemed like yesterday that this young convict had flown into Heathrow airport for a first taste of the Motherland. Like a stopped clock, everything seemed to have stood still since the day I arrived as a teenager, wet behind the ears, eager to experience the UK to its fullest. The vast green fields, rows of identical houses, and masses of London traffic were all as I remembered them. Nothing had changed, except that this time, arriving for the 1997 Ashes tour, I had a few more quid in my pocket, a little less puppy fat around my cheeks and my cover drive and pull shot should have marginally improved. Initial impressions are so significant. Everything seems so untouched and unchanged every time I fly in to the swarming concrete monstrosity of Heathrow airport. The heavy, frosty air, grey skies, red double-decker buses, black cabs, white complexions, pints of warm beer, rain and . . . rush, rush, rush.

In the blink of an eye, four thousand and something days may have passed by, yet the memories of that introductory five-week, cricket-playing, pint-drinking tour up and down the English motorways as a schoolboy instilled a burning ambition to play professional cricket in England. What could be better than playing this infatuating game day in, day out, and getting paid for the pleasure?

A seed had been planted the moment our tour manager stood at the front of our team's luxury coach and warned us that this thirty-five-day tour would be exciting but also very tiring. With twenty-eight games of cricket and seven rest or travel days we would soon learn what it would be like to be a full-time cricketer. For this aspiring professional cricket junkie it seemed as close to heaven on earth as you could get.

In five weeks I learnt that English cricket was fun, the social life a riot, the beer warm and the camaraderie of a cricket changing-room an inspiring blast. No matter what it took, I was going to have a piece of this lifestyle on a more permanent basis. Maybe I could actually be a cricketer when I grew up rather than a train driver, a phys-ed teacher or a car salesman. The question was, how was I going to do it?

As my sporting career became reality (much to my mum's horror – she kept asking me up until a year or so ago when I was going to get a real job) it became apparent that the only way to live my dream of playing cricket every day of the year was to play some pretty damn good cricket along the way. So I set out in pursuit of step one, international cricket. I figured that the only way to play cricket all year round, including a stint of county cricket, was to play for Australia. As this is possibly the only undeniable method of recognition by the English county administrators, it was the only way to go.

Now I am someone who simply loves cricket: I always have done, and I still do. Since I was about five years old (perhaps even younger), I have been playing backyard Test matches with my brothers, Adam and Jono, and sister Jemma. Every summer, under the heavenly blue skies in Perth, I would pretend to be Allan Border, Kim Hughes, Rodney Marsh or Dennis Lillee. We would play cricket along the driveway, in or out of the swimming pool or along the beach, from dawn to dusk, every day. Unless we were sick, there wouldn't be a day go by without an Ashes Test series running rampant in the Langer household.

On my twenty-first birthday, Don Lee, my next door neighbour in the first house we lived in, told me that when I was five years old I used to brag that I was going have a green baggy Australian cricket cap one day. I hadn't seen Don for years, but I remember that every Saturday morning he would roll the lawn mower down to the local park and cut out a cricket pitch for all the kids in the neighbourhood. That was my introduction to semi-competitive cricket, as we played cricket against all the big kids around the area. No matter what happened, Don says I just couldn't get enough of the game. With a big smile he reminded me of my early bragging and told me that it didn't surprise him that I had finally earned that precious baggy green cap.

It is a strange experience when your childhood heroes become your team-mates. After progressing through the normal ranks of under-age club and school cricket in Perth, I was lucky to be selected, as a fifteen-year-old, to play my debut first-grade game for Scarborough Cricket Club. To my delight, D.K. Lillee was playing for Scarborough, and we were playing against Subiaco Floreat, with Kim Hughes and Terry Alderman.

Although it was a little daunting, it was an amazing

experience. As a youngster I used to pretend to be these guys who I was now playing with and against. Can you imagine, I walked out to bat in my first-grade debut, past Dennis Lillee who wished me good luck, and onto the ground where Terry Alderman was at the end of his run-up about to bowl to me. Kim Hughes, my absolute childhood hero, was standing in the slips behind me and I was taking guard. It was almost like a dream, but an incredible buzz.

After that first England tour, and with a couple of first-grade seasons under my belt, I was keen to leave University for a year and play club cricket in the UK. With little experience of English cricket, I asked spin legend Tony Lock for some advice. Tony was working at the WACA as a coach and when I asked him he told me to leave it with him. Within a few days Tony had called me back with the news that he had set me up with a club called Old Millhillians in North London.

Now that is a story in itself!

The day before I left for my six-month sojourn, I was sitting at home having a family barbecue, when I received a phone call from Tony Lock. After wishing me good luck his voice changed into a more stern tone. 'Justin, the gentleman you will be staying with for the first few days is Nigel Wray. He will pick you up from the airport. Now Justin, it is very important that you are extremely polite to him. Call him Mr Wray and be on your very best behaviour. He is a very wealthy man who will look after you while you are in England, but I cannot stress enough how important it is for you to be on your best behaviour.'

I had the message loud and clear!

After ringing the Wray household from a public

phone in Athens, where I had stopped over for a week, I was cut off just as I had said I would see him at the airport at 9.30 p.m. The whole flight to Heathrow I had nightmares of turning up to this busy foreign airport to find no one waiting for me. The mind plays terrible games with you in moments of nervous agitation. When the moment of truth arrived, I need never have worried, as the first sign I saw when I walked through the gates was a big card with the name JUSTIN LANGER staring me right in the face.

There he was, just as I had imagined him, exactly how he had sounded on the phone. Short, bald, grinning from ear to ear, exactly how I imagined a 'wealthy, sugar daddy, English gentleman'. Nervously I approached him, extended my hand and said, 'Mr Wray it is an absolute pleasure to meet you, sir.' My manners were exquisite, I mean I had really outdone myself this time. Mr Wray just smiled at me, picked up my bags for me and took me out to the brand new Land Rover.

I remember it was pouring with rain, a great introduction to English weather, but for the hour-long journey I chattered away. I felt very comfortable and he simply continued to smile. Just as we pulled up to the heavy wooden electric gates of this magnificent English mansion known as The Priory, Mr Wray looked at me straight in the face and said: 'Justin, I guess you must have realised by now I am Mr Wray's chauffeur, Ron. It has been a pleasure meeting you and if there is anything I can do to make you feel at home don't be afraid to ask.'

I couldn't believe it; I had been done. No wonder Ron had been grinning from ear to ear for the last hour or so.

This meant I had to go through this nervous greeting once again.

As I opened the door to the most beautiful house I have ever seen, there, standing in the hallway, was this tall, fit man with long dark hair and a caring smile on his face. This time it was Mr Wray who came up and extended his hand saying, 'Hello Justin, my name is Nigel Wray. Welcome to my house, please make yourself at home and if there is anything you need just ask and we will look after it for you.'

I was dumbfounded, he definitely didn't look like I expected and when I called him Mr Wray, he just laughed and told me that Nigel would be fine and that Mr Wray made him feel old – he was only forty.

From that moment a great friendship was formed and, although I hate to admit it, it was actually this Englishman who has had a strong influence on my moderate success to this point.

After an amazing night's sleep, in a bed that I needed a step ladder to get into, I decided to have a look around The Priory and see if it was really as big as it had seemed the night before. I had only reached the steps leading down into the main part of the house, when an attractive blonde lady and a young girl greeted me. After the previous night's fiasco with the chauffeur I couldn't help but wonder who these people were. Before I could speak, Linda and Lucy Wray introduced themselves as the wife and daughter of Nigel. What a relief, and what a thrill: these people actually seemed like normal people, not the posh, rich family that Tony Lock had suggested.

My shyness quickly turned into enthusiasm as I learnt what the Old Millhillians Cricket Club had in store for me for the next six months. The first step was to find a place for me to stay because The Priory was only a temporary resting place until I got myself on my feet. The plan was to stay with the other Australian who was teaching at Mill Hill College and playing for the OMs on the weekends.

After a couple of days living in luxury, my first meeting with John Hurley was arranged. I rang the door bell and walked into what was going to be my home for the next six months. Wow! This was something else. 'Hurls' was sitting on his couch watching *The Blues Brothers* for the forty-seventh time. In one corner there was a pile of pizza boxes stacked to the roof (a competition apparently), in the middle of the table was a Bundy rum umbrella, and there were dishes everywhere. The whole apartment was about as big as the bedroom I had been sleeping in until this encounter.

This was going to be interesting. All sorts of thoughts screamed through my mind, not least of them being 'Where's my mum'! After meeting Hurls, though, I started to relax. Maybe this would be a good start to my manhood. Living in the ultimate bachelor pad would surely mean a rapid introduction to life away from my mum. Yes, I thought, this will toughen me up a bit and I would go home a much more worldly person. I would go home a man – if I could survive this I could survive anything.

After setting up a time to move in to my new home, I heard the door bell ring. There at the front door was Linda, ready to pick me up from my home for the next six months. I shook Hurl's hand and said, 'I'll see you tomorrow, mate, I'll bring all my things over in the morning.'

That morning never came!

As I opened the door, Linda nearly fainted. As she later explained, she had heard about the place, but until now she had never seen it. Politely she smiled and spent the journey home apologising. 'You poor baby, we can't let you live there, we will just have to find you somewhere else to live, you leave it up to me.' I tried to convince her, obviously not too convincingly, that it would be a great life experience, a great growing-up adventure, but luckily she wouldn't have it.

We kept looking and looking for a place for me to stay for the next six months, but unfortunately we just couldn't find anyone else to take me. This meant that I had to endure six months of luxury at The Priory. Yippee!!

What a six months it was; the generosity and friendship were amazing. To this day I am still bewildered how they put up with me for so long. It is a time I will never forget.

Nigel Wray is a great teacher in his own funny sort of way. He probably doesn't realise it, but he really has had an amazing influence on my life until now. For the wealth he has accumulated through his diverse businesses, he leads a pretty simple life. He could be forgiven for leading a flamboyant lifestyle but that is not his way.

During my time in England with the Wrays and the OMs I experienced a great shock about three months into the season. It felt like I had been hit by a brick wall, the brick wall being Nigel.

As usual I was chatting about this and that, but specifically about what he thought were the most important traits of the successful people he had met or read about.

He was giving me the answers to all my questions and talking me through his ideas of why he thought he had done so well in business. The usual things came up: perseverance, hard work, determination, dedication, sacrifice, discipline, self belief and so on. I was getting all inspired, generally pumped up and feeling good about myself, when from out of the blue I was knocked out by the best right hook I had ever seen. Not an actual right hook, of course, but something that felt just as bad.

Nigel pulled over in his car, looked at me and said, 'While we are on the subject there are a few things I would like to talk to you about. As far as I am concerned, I am afraid you don't possess any of the things I have been talking about. Sure you talk a good game, you keep saying that you want to be a Test cricketer and yes you do have some talent, but I haven't seen anything yet to indicate that you will make it to the top.'

I couldn't believe it. My jaw hit the car floor and for once in my life I was lost for words. As far as I was concerned I had been making plenty of runs for his club and was a bit of a star. Everyone at the club was telling me what a good player I was and I guess I just believed it.

He went on, 'I have been watching you. I have never seen you do any extra training, no extra running, no extra work at all. To be an elite sportsman surely you have to have an elite and superior level of fitness to everyone else. Your preparation is poor, you are out until all hours drinking at pubs and nightclubs. You are playing a fairly average level of cricket and while you are making a lot of runs you aren't making anywhere near the amount of runs I would expect you to be making. You are making silly mistakes on and off the field, and to me this is just an indication of your attitude and the lifestyle you are leading. You're not showing the discipline I would expect from a future Test cricketer. Remember it is not whether you have talent, it is what you do with the talent that makes all the difference. You should be looking to dominate the level you are at, and looking to be constantly improving. I wouldn't say you are exactly dominating here and constantly improving, would you?'

I was shattered. It pretty much came out of the blue. Until that moment I had no idea what Nigel had thought of me. We had been getting along like a house on fire, I was living in his house and I was feeling a part of the family. At the time I really thought I was doing OK. It dawned on me that I better have a good hard look at myself in the mirror. That night I went home and wrote in my diary about the day's events. I concluded with the words, 'Nigel Wray reckons I won't make it, I'll show that bastard.'

From that day on my attitude changed completely. It was like Rocky Balboa's boxing coach telling him that he was fat, slow, lazy and good for nothing. Old Mick, Rocky's coach, said, 'Apollo Creed was going to murder him in the ring unless he got off his backside and started clicking into gear.'

Nigel's rocket had exactly the same effect on me. From that day I started training harder than I had ever trained before. I was running, doing weights, swimming, skipping, saying 'No' more often when people asked me to go out drinking and partying, and generally focusing on what I had been talking so much about.

Today I am very glad that Nigel took the time to tell me the truth, even if at the time it hurt to hear it. His encouragement ever since then has been unbelievable. After that day in the car, Nigel always promised me that if I continued to work hard and was lucky enough to play Test cricket then he would be there to watch my first Test, no matter where it was in the world. The day I left England I reminded him of his promise and he just smiled and said, 'A promise is a promise!'

History will say that I played my first Test match for Australia against the West Indies in 1993. History will also tell you that I found out about my first Test selection only twenty-four hours before I was due to walk out onto the beautiful Adelaide Oval. As the match progressed through the first day, I was 0 not out overnight. After a restless and nervous night's sleep I had a shower, breakfast and took the elevator downstairs to where the team bus was waiting to take us to the ground. As I stepped out of the lift and walked towards the reception desk I thought I must have been hallucinating. There, standing at the reception of the Hindley Park Royal, was my friend, my mentor and that bastard Nigel Wray.

It was one of the most amazing acts of faith I have ever experienced. Most incredible was the fact that he had dropped everything at home, and within such short notice had got onto a plane and travelled to the other side of the world. On arriving at the Adelaide airport he hailed a taxi and asked the Italian taxi driver to take him to a nice hotel somewhere in town. He had no idea that we were staying at this particular hotel, but simply took the advice of the driver.

Incredibly he was checking in to the hotel at the

moment I was walking through reception. I simply couldn't believe it. Call it luck, call it fate, call it whatever you like, but it was a great moment in my life. He had made a promise and he had kept it. He had inspired me, pulled me into line a couple of years beforehand, and had been there at one of the best days of my life. It was simply unbelievable.

The funny thing was that after the Test match we were having dinner and Nigel said to me, 'Remember that day in the car when we had a talk about a few things to do with your goal of playing for Australia?'

How could I forget?

'Well, can you also remember writing in your diary that I will show that bastard?'

Once again my jaw hit the ground. 'How did you know about that?'

He finished, 'You left it open on your bed one day and Linda saw it lying there. She sneaked a look at what you had written. For once in my life I am happy to be thought of as a bastard.'

I couldn't believe it, the man is full of surprises.

Funnily enough, one of the other people who was at that first Test match was John Hurley who had flown from Sydney to be there. He had obviously forgiven me for not moving in with him and he and I have been friends ever since that season in England.

After my English experience and with international selection achieved, I arrived at Heathrow airport, as proud as a little boy with his first blue ribbon, in the summer of 1997. Clad in the green and gold striped blazer my initial attentions were solely directed towards destroying English cricket, beating the 'poms', and retaining those inestimable and precious Ashes.

I couldn't help but admire my team-mates Warne, Waugh, McGrath and Taylor lapping up the limelight of the ravenous English press.

After a tentative start to the tour, the Ashes were retained and even though I played little part in the on-field success, it was still a special tour for me. Not only do I treasure wonderful memories of a fantastic three months in England but it also gave me an opportunity for two introductions of great consequence. The first one was at Buckingham Palace, where the team was invited for a cup of tea with Her Majesty Queen Elizabeth. Undoubtedly, this was one of the great thrills of my life. As she entered the room, the hair on the back of my neck stood on end, sending an excited shiver to every cell in my body. Imagine meeting the Queen! This extraordinary person actually smiled at my colleagues and me, and chatted to us as if we were her closest friends. Who would ever believe it?

The second encounter was a brief conversation with Middlesex captain Mark Ramprakash. After England had won the final Test match at The Oval, 'Ramps' introduced himself over a diet coke and a friendship was initiated. While Ramps may not have inspired the same initial emotional ado as had meeting the Queen, his introduction was more significant and just as exciting.

Could the seed of hope, stored away somewhere within the grey matter beneath my skull, be about to mature and blossom into reality?

Sitting in The Oval changing-room, we discussed the prospect of a short, left-handed Aussie opener playing county cricket for a season. Being a realist (sometimes),

I knew the chances of this happening were slim, as I had hardly set the world on fire over the last three months. As the beer started to flow and the blow of a crushing fifth Test defeat began to soften, the memories of my meeting with Ramps also started to fade into obscurity. It was time to enjoy the fruits of a relatively successful 1997 Australian touring team to England, and briefly forget cricket for a while.

Sunday, 17 October 1997 – reality bites

My faded memory automatically flooded back to crystal clarity when the squealing of my telephone rocked me out of a deep sleep one Sunday night early in our Australian summer. Rolling over and picking up the phone, my eyes quickly shot open and my mind went into overdrive as the voice on the other end introduced itself as Mark Ramprakash. The seed was about to have its second watering in a couple of months. A five-minute conversation was ended by Ramps.

'Well, I'm glad to hear you still may be interested. We are looking at a few prospects but we will be in touch one way or the other within the next week or so. Good luck for the rest of the season.'

Luckily, our domestic season was just under way so I had plenty to keep my mind off the prospect of an English summer, or that is what I thought. For two weeks I was like a teenager waiting for the results of final exams. At last the caller on the other end of the phone was the one I had been eagerly waiting for. The chairman of the Middlesex cricket committee, Bob Gale, finally rang me to give me the good news.

'Justin we are thrilled to be able to offer you a contract for next season. Please go away and think about it and get back to me within the next few weeks.'

The next few weeks – are you kidding? Send me the contract and I will sign it right away. I'm not missing this opportunity for anything.

'No worries, Bob. I will weigh it all up and phone you back with a definite answer in the next few weeks. Your offer sounds reasonable. Thank you and I look forward to speaking to you soon.'

Who do you think I was trying to kid? I suppose I have to sound like a professional, knowing exactly what I'm doing. In reality, he can't send me the contract soon enough but I can't sound too keen. Isn't that one of the rules of negotiation?

Monday, 18 October 1997 – the next day!

Bugger the rules of negotiation!

'Bob, I have had enough time to think about it. I would love to play for Middlesex. The offer sounds very fair. I hope I can help you guys next season. You have a deal.'

Yippee! I feel like jumping up and down. The seed truly is about to blossom.

Like most cricketers, I have always dreamed of making

a century at Lord's, the Mecca of cricket. Obviously a Test century would be the perfect occasion, but ever since I played a friendly for the Old Millhillians on the Lord's nursery ground in 1989 this ambition has continued to grow. Who will ever forget Michael Slater's Test century at Lord's? His reaction was exactly what I would expect from a young Australian making his first Test hundred at the home of cricket. Pure elation! Pure adrenalin! Pure pride!

Now the prospect of this young Australian batting at Lord's is coming closer to reality. In six months' time, I will be a full-time cricket professional – a season for Middlesex, my home ground Lord's, living in London, a young family, a new adventure, a dream come true. You wouldn't be dead for quids, would you?

So much has been said about the English system of cricket, I am going into this English summer with a very open mind. Until I have experienced the system first-hand, I am not in a position to comment, but by the end of this long summer that may well change. One thing's for sure, I am going to have one hell of a time checking it out.

CHAPTER ONE
The First Fixture

Tuesday, 14 April – welcome to England

'Ladies and gentlemen we have now started our descent into a cloudy and cold London Heathrow airport. The time is currently 5.45 a.m. and the ground temperature is 3° Celsius. We should have you disembarking on time, at five minutes past six. From my staff and I, we thank you for flying Cathay Pacific and look forward to seeing you next time you fly with us. We hope you have a pleasant stay in London.'

This time it is different. The lines of houses, green fields and horrendous traffic remain the same, but this time I am not here as an Aussie determined to beat the poms. This time I am in London as an invited guest of the Middlesex County Cricket Club. I am one of 'them', or one of 'you' depending upon whose eyes are reading this diary. I am happy and excited about the prospect of county cricket; this should be a fantastic experience.

Since signing with Middlesex, I have had a recurring and vivid nightmare about today. Ever since that phone call from Bob Gale, I haven't been able to shake off my greatest fear, until now. The nightmare wasn't about county bowlers, golden ducks or traffic jams. It was more frightening than any of these. The nightmare was simply how are we going to get through a twenty-hour flight with a one-year-old, beautiful but energetic baby girl? Perth to London is a long and potentially embarrassing haul. People are paying their hard-earned cash to reach a far-off destination. The last thing they need is a screaming baby ruining what is already a tough assignment. I know the feeling because I have been on the other end of the stick many times before.

Please God, make this as painless as possible!

You know that intimidating reaction you get when you walk up the aisle of the plane carrying a baby. Everyone sees you coming and prays that you are not sitting next to them. At first you get the lowered eyebrows and crossed fingers and toes, then you feel the heavy sighs of relief as you pass by each passenger. Looking over your shoulder, it is amazing how those previously cringing patrons suddenly swap their grimaces for affectionate but relieved smiles. I have often felt like sitting down in every spare seat just to tease each one of those frowning customers.

Please God, I will be good and say my prayers if you just help me out here. I need a bit of help and I know if anyone can do it, you can.

Worry should never have weighed me down; my little girl took to the Hong Kong to London journey as she may later take to a colourfully wrapped Easter egg. In fact, of the fourteen-hour second leg, Jess slept for a marathon twelve of those taxing hours. We even survived the pressure pains which affect little babies' ears on the descent into Heathrow airport. What a bloody champion!

Thank you, my friend! You may never understand just what a relief Jess's effort was for my wife Sue, our second unborn and yours truly.

You know when you were a little kid and on a cold winter morning you pretended to smoke a cigarette by breathing out a line of smoke every time you opened your frozen lips? That's what it was like as we stepped off the plane into the morning air. It is freezing in our temporary homeland. Those pretend smoke hazes indicate that it really is very cold. Could this be an ominous sign for the summer or is it just a normal April morning? Just forty-eight hours ago, I was walking on Scarborough beach enjoying a 30° summer's afternoon in Perth.

My initial impression is that this will take some getting used to! At our new address we were greeted by a Sky television cameraman, central heating inside and a 4° temperature out. Wow! With a Sheffield Shield season completed only a fortnight ago, the reality of a new season and a new challenge is dawning on me. You would think we might have a little time to settle into our flat, the same one occupied in the past by Desmond Haynes, Jacques Kallis and Dion Nash. Not a chance of course, the season was under way the moment we stepped off the plane. Without a ball being bowled, the reality of professional cricket and its many facets is evident.

The questions have begun already. What do you

think is wrong with English cricket? Why is the English cricket team so bad? Why is Australian cricket so strong? Do we play too much cricket in this country? What is the Australian Cricket Academy like? How are you going to help Middlesex?

Typical questions which I am sure will become easier to answer as the summer progresses. My general answer to most of the English problems is, 'Let me play a full season of county cricket and then I will be able to make a judgement.' Having watched England's progress since they lost the Ashes in 1989, I have some views on their game, but these will develop – and may even change. They will certainly be highlighted in this diary account of an English summer. With next winter's Australian Ashes series and the 1999 World Cup evolving as two of the biggest events in English cricket, it will be exciting to see how their campaign develops.

Wednesday, 15 April – first day for the new boy

My first training session with the club down at the Finchley indoor nets was always going to be an exciting experience, although there were a few butterflies flying around inside my two T-shirts, sweatshirt, tracksuit top and sleeveless cricket vest. It is still bloody cold. When I walked through the front doors, it almost felt like that first kiss with your high-school sweetheart. My palms were a bit clammy, my mouth a little dry and my legs something like two sticks of half-set jelly. Luckily, Mike Gatting was the first familiar face I saw. Sitting drinking a mug of coffee and doing his mandatory daily crossword, he jumped up from his seat, smiled his broad friendly grin, extended his little stubby hand and welcomed me to the club.

'A bit cold for you, is it, Master? You'd better get used to it little fella, there's plenty more of this to come,' he smiled. 'That Middlesex sweater looks good on you. Welcome to the club, we should have a lot of fun.'

With this, he was back to his crossword, a hobby, I found out later in the season, that was as much a part of his daily routine as sitting down on 'the throne', eating a bacon sandwich or picking up his favourite cricket bat. Mike Gatting is Mr Middlesex and if first impressions are anything to go by, he and I will get on famously this summer.

The Middlesex team are a great bunch of guys. While training was only light in the indoor nets, it looks like there is a pretty good core of talent to choose from. Although I missed the pre-season training camp in Portugal, it is obvious that spirits are high from their week in the sun. Everyone is having a joke about 'Thommo forgetting his passport', 'Gunner falling asleep on the bar' and 'Buck dancing like John Travolta on the restaurant table'. This is great to see; from my experience, a happy team is generally a successful team.

On the cricket front, the season promises to be a ripper. I am seriously looking forward to it all.

After training, Middlesex secretary Vinnie Codrington invited John Buchanan ('Buck'), Middlesex's new Aussie coach, and me for an afternoon in the fresh London air. With my jetlagged eyes poking out of my head like a couple of bursting ping-pong balls and my head beating like an African bongo drum, I should have been a little more sensible and politely declined the offer. Being eager to impress, though, it was hard to refuse my first invitation in London. It was to watch rugby, not my ideal afternoon out, especially as I know the rules of the game about as well as I know the rules of motherhood. Coming from the West Coast of Australia, I can tell you everything about Aussie Rules football but my knowledge of rugby stops with Michael Lynagh, David Campese, John Eales and some team called the All Blacks.

The first half was a torrid affair slugged out in the mud; the second half was less torrid, or so they tell me. A huge black cloud and an extreme drop in temperature enticed Buck and me to a cowardly escape from the cold and rain. To say it was cold is an understatement. It was absolutely freezing. My theory on the cold is that there is no point being a hero, so it didn't take much coaxing from my new coach to persuade me to adjourn to the Richmond clubhouse.

Although we missed the final forty minutes, we made up for it by meeting a few of the locals and drinking a couple of pints of the local brew; purely an exercise in warming up the insides of course! By the time we left the clubhouse, we were both well and truly loose and warmed up, and while I was fighting the jetlagged eyes I was feeling as though I was now an expert on the problems of English cricket and English sport in general.

As I am sure I'll find out during the summer, there are always plenty of experts in the bar. It is always so much easier from behind the fence, sitting in the grandstand, or even better still, in the warmth of the clubhouse with a pint in your hand.

It is amazing how many experts there are around the place. If nothing else, it makes for most entertaining listening as the problems magnify and the solutions simplify with every pint emptied. It was classic afternoon entertainment, especially for two Aussies introducing themselves to British culture.

Thursday, 16 April – snow, snow, snow!

My new team-mates must be wondering who the hell this lunatic from Australia thinks he is. Dancing around in the snow, laughing and yipping like I have just won the national lottery, admittedly must have been confusing for my London colleagues, who started taking photos like Japanese tourists. The thing is, this is a fantastic experience for me; I have never seen snow before, other than on the TV of course. For three hours, thick, white, beautiful snow fell on the streets of London – not great news for the start of the cricket season tomorrow, but one hell of an experience nonetheless. Living in sleepy Perth where the skies are blue and the ocean water warm, the closest I have been to snow is the ice-cream freezer at the local supermarket. Buck is in the same boat. He lives in Brisbane where the coldest day is possibly Britain's hottest in the peak of summer.

Can you imagine a couple of Aussies turning up at Uxbridge cricket club for our first outdoor training session in England, and before a ball could be bowled, the snow came tumbling down. It was an unreal scenario for me. I walked into my first net session dressed in thermal 'undies', two T-shirts, long and sleeveless cricket jumpers and a blue Hill Samuel raincoat. The pitch was so green and soft that it resembled a bowling green rather than a cricket pitch, and as I took strike for my first ball as a county cricketer, I couldn't help but laugh at the snow building up on the peak of my new Middlesex helmet.

What have I got myself in for here? This isn't cricket weather. Surely I should be lying on a leopard-skin rug in front of an open fire, sipping red wine and cuddling my wife, on a day like this. Shouldn't I?

My shivering biceps and chattering teeth weren't so much a result of Angus Fraser and Richard Johnson running in to bowl to me on the sawdust-laden pitch, but rather a consequence of the sheer cold in the air.

What did surprise me was Angus Fraser's attitude to his training. It is no wonder he is one of the most consistent competitors English cricket has produced. Even though he has just returned from a successful tour of the West Indies, 'Gus' was straight off his long run-up, bowling as if every ball could be his last. Most bowlers would complain about the soft run-ups, the wet crease or the slippery balls, but not Angus Fraser. He was straight into it. A bit of sawdust, a new ball and he was as happy as a fat spider, running in to bowl at this left-handed Aussie trying to make an impression on his adopted team-mates. Gus loves bowling, simple as that, and every opportunity he gets he is into it. I think it is this admirable characteristic that has helped him to the levels he is now attaining.

To say the first few balls were an alarming awakening would be something of an understatement. This pudding of a pitch, as they call it over here, took some getting used to. Foreign to these conditions, I expected every ball to rear at me like a striking cobra. Surprisingly, it played a lot easier than expected, with short balls sitting up to be pulled or cut and the fuller balls simply hitting a length and ballooning into my straight bat. Every now and then, one of Angus Fraser's good-length balls reared up and knocked the snow off the peak of my helmet, but generally I was pleasantly surprised at the way this type of pitch plays. Never judge a book by its cover? If nothing else, the many varying conditions I am sure to encounter this summer will make me a better player come September.

I was not the only one trying to make an impression today. The new coach wasn't going to let anything, even a downpour of snow, ruin his first, planned, outdoor session. He had the full squad running around like penguins, catching, throwing and fielding for a couple of hours. I don't think the Middlesex guys know what has hit them. It would have been easy to finish the session before it even started and I got the feeling the usual procedure on a day like this would have been an adjournment to the clubhouse for hot tea and biscuits.

It sounds like a pretty good idea to me. My fingers are freezing and every time the ball hits them they start singing like Pavarotti on a bad day. I can see what Buck is trying to do; a good idea to instil discipline early, but maybe I can slip off without anyone noticing?

Instead of this, Buck decided to lay down the law from day one. I think it is the best thing he could have done. I put on a brave, tough Aussie image of loving this extra work in the snow and rain, but in reality you know what I was thinking.

When the session finally came to an end, the talk in the hot showers provided me with immense entertainment.

'JL, what is Buck doing? Is he crazy or something? All this is going to do is give us pneumonia. Do you reckon he knows what he's doing?'

'I wish I was still in Portugal,' came another cry.

'My hands are killing me. I could have pulled a hamstring out there,' came from someone else. Over all these whinges boomed a strong voice coming from the end shower.

'Stop complaining. It will do you the world of good putting in some extra work. It is exactly what you guys need, a bit of toughening up. Get on with it and stop your whining.'

Mr Middlesex had spoken the words I would have loved to have said, but had diplomatically kept to myself so as not to ruin all friendships at this stage of my Middlesex career. Luckily, it is pre-season and by the time everyone was warm again, the spirits were still high with everyone feeling as though something had been achieved on this miserable first day in the open air.

I hope it gets a bit warmer than this. One of my biggest hates is cold. I could be in for a rude shock!

Following training, Buck and I must have looked like a couple of excited schoolkids, jumping around, smiling and laughing, throwing snowballs at each other for over an hour. We have been complaining about the wet and cold of England, but the heavier the snow fell, the more fun we had. While it was no big deal for everyone else, we made the most of this, hopefully, one-off experience of the summer.

Friday, 17 April – a damp start

Day one of the 1998 County Championship season and all the expectation, energy and fire of a new season was literally extinguished today by continual rain at Canterbury in Kent. After the pre-season camp in Portugal, indoor nets, gym work and preparatory meetings, my new Middlesex team-mates were raring to get the season under way. Unfortunately, the start of the county season resembled more of a winter's day at Old Trafford. A clash between Manchester United and Arsenal would have been more appropriate than the cricket season opener between Kent and Middlesex. There were puddles all over the waterlogged ground, blue plastic covers over the huge centre square, and spectators wearing raincoats, gloves and beanie hats.

Luckily, I was presented with a new Middlesex beanie yesterday, and a pack of magic hand-warming socks, an invention which could become my best friend if this weather continues. Whoever invented this device is a bloody marvel! It works like a heatpack sitting in your pocket. The more you touch it, the hotter it gets and the warmer your ice-block hands become. In fact, it acts by thawing out your fingers, in a way not dissimilar to wrapping your hands around a hot cup of Nana's veggie soup. A fantastic relief! As a cricketer, freezing fingers are one of the worst fears. Have you ever had a brand new cricket ball slap into your hands on a day like this? Mate, there is nothing worse! Firstly, you know that it is going to hurt, so you generally go at it half-heartedly, a big mistake in itself. Then, when the ball does eventually arrive, the pain is like a thousand hungry bees stinging away at your fingertips. 'Mr Handwarmer' inventor, whoever he is, should be inducted into cricket's hall of fame. If it wasn't for his invention, I am sure a lot of cricketers would fake an injury until June or July when the sun decides to shows its pretty face. All he has to do now is invent something that keeps your inside thigh and backside warm when you're batting. If your fingers don't hurt enough, you should feel the pain of a cricket ball thumping into a cold inside thigh, or flicking your bum on its way through to the keeper. Just thinking about it makes me grimace.

The cold and rain didn't limit itself to Canterbury. The whole of the country proved generally cricketless today. West Indian superstar Courtney Walsh, who plays for Gloucester, was pictured standing at fine leg wearing three or four sweaters, towel wrapped around his shoulders and head, frowning and hugging his arms to his chest like he was hugging his long-lost girlfriend. It really is miserable. Spare a thought for us here in freezing England.

How does Courtney keep doing it? Maybe it is just for the money, maybe he just loves playing cricket? On days like this, with his big, lean frame, he must be suffering. The man is a superstar; how his body stands up year in, year out is one of the marvels of modern day sport.

The only exciting cricket news making the press today was the big story that Brian Lara was caught behind for a duck in his first innings as captain of Warwickshire.

The ironic part of his early dismissal was that it was against Durham, the team he scored 501 against three seasons ago.

I wonder how B.C. Lara will fare this summer. He is another player who has played so much cricket in the last decade. I wonder whether it ever takes its toll. I will look forward to catching up with him later in the season.

Saturday, 18 April – killing time

Rain again last night and those wet patches on the Canterbury pitch don't look any drier. Canterbury cricket ground, beautiful as it is, looks more like a Swiss ski resort than a county cricket venue today. Both umpires were keen to play at all costs so we had a very long day waiting around in the dressing-rooms. The umpires, admirably enthusiastic at the day's prospects, don't have to face Kent's pace attack on this wet, green pitch.

If freezing fingers are one of the players' top pet hates, sitting around a changing-room is an equal contender. Today is very reminiscent of the start of last year's Ashes tour, when wet weather dogged the start of the trip. There are only so many games of cards you can play, and even though there are so many varying newspapers in England, there is only so much news that your brain can digest in one sitting.

Fortunately, the indoor facilities at Canterbury were available for a few throw downs for the batsmen, a bit of fielding and a handful of overs for the bowlers. To tell you the truth, it was great to be inside in the warmth practising. Outside is that cold, your ears sting and your hands feel like ice-blocks; not all that much fun for a man used to spending the first month of a cricket season in shorts, T-shirts and sun cream.

Despite the damp and dicey-looking pitch and the ugly and angry black clouds creeping ominously behind the pavilion, the umpires, in their wisdom, decided that the game should begin. After more discussion than a political debate, Middlesex lost the toss and the first ball of our 1998 county season was finally delivered at 4.30 p.m. on day two by English paceman Dean Headley to yours truly.

Only seven overs were bowled followed by more heavy rain, more covers and more frustration. Luckily, a few viciously rising deliveries by Headley and Martin McCague rocketed into my ribs warming me up as quickly as a Mike Tyson right hook splatters the nose of an unworthy opponent.

I would rather be out in the middle than sitting in the changing-room any day, but I have to admit it is days like this which leave you questioning your desire to be an opening batsman. Hopefully this type of day won't be indicative of the season. Time will tell!

Sunday, 19 April – how many one-day games?

Today I realised first hand what everyone means when they say English cricketers play so much cricket in a season. Throughout this summer, we will play a forty-over, Sunday League, one-day fixture in the middle of every first-class game. To an Aussie unused to this intensity, it seems quite extraordinary. After the first two days of our first four-day championship match, we moved onto another pitch for today's forty-over fixture. Tomorrow and Tuesday we are back into championship mode and will complete the already commenced four-day match. That's plenty of cricket, even for the most ardent cricket lover.

The wicket at Canterbury is a classic English cricket pitch or pudding, very similar to the one I was introduced to during my first net session at Uxbridge the other day – slow, green and sodden after a week's rainfall. Add to that a short boundary on one side, the famous Canterbury tree which sits inside the boundary ropes, and a lush green yet lightning-fast outfield, and you have a typical English setting for a game of cricket.

Forty-over cricket is a new experience for me. Played on a Sunday afternoon with a white ball and coloured clothing, it is really no different from the fifty-over affair we are used to back home. Unfortunately, today finished controversially as a result of the Duckworth-Lewis scoring system for rain-affected one-day games. This was devised by two statisticians and has been in use in England since 1997.

Chasing 207, Kent were always behind the target after excellent bowling spells from Angus Fraser and Jamie Hewitt. Despite a typically classy innings from Kent's overseas player Carl Hooper, Middlesex always looked in a strong position to win the game. When the rain came tumbling down in the bleak, late-afternoon conditions, Kent were 115 for 3 with twelve overs remaining. According to the ground announcer and the paperwork in captain Mark Ramprakash's pocket, the game at this stage was to be declared a tie – arguably a fair result – if we decided to come off the ground. Unfortunately for Middlesex, the Duckworth-Lewis system, unbeknown to us, had Kent winning the match by 0.73 of a run. Work that one out. If you can, you're a better mathematician than I am. Archimedes, Pythagoras, Newton or Einstein may have had trouble calculating this result.

It was a farce really, the second time in six months I have played in a side robbed of victory by a computer system. Last Aussie summer we were 200 for 1 at the MCG but the computer ruled the Western Warriors losers to Victoria, despite having nine wickets and seven overs in hand, and only a handful of runs to score. You have to have rules and guidelines, no one will argue with that, but surely there is room for common sense in cricket administration.

Is there a better system? It is very hard to find a fair solution in these matters, ultimately because cricket can be so unpredictable, but in a case like today I believe common sense should prevail. These competitions are worth a lot of money and esteem for the county clubs and every point can be vital at the end of the summer. It will be interesting to see whether today's result proves to be a costly one thanks to the computer.

Monday, 20 April – a convict's view

Covered with hessian all day yesterday, the wet patches on a good length hadn't really dried any more than we witnessed on Saturday. In fact, both ends lent assistance to Kent's first-class attack led by England paceman Dean Headley, Aussie-born Martin McCague, rookie speedster Ben Phillips and England one-day specialists Mark Ealham and Matthew Fleming. On another freezing cold day at Canterbury, my team-mates fought hard to secure one bonus point against arguably the best county attack in England.

The system of points scoring is different from Shield cricket. No points are scored for winning on the first innings; instead a bonus point is scored at 200, another at 250, 300 and 350. After 120 overs, no points can be obtained regardless of the situation. On the bowling side, taking nine or ten wickets gives the maximum of four points. One point for three wickets, two points for five wickets, three points for seven wickets. For an outright victory, another sixteen points go to the winners, giving a maximum of twenty-four points available for every game.

Since this is the first four-day game of the summer, I reserve judgement about this scoring system, but first impressions are that it makes for positive and attacking cricket.

Keep putting on a brave face JL. Aussies are meant to be tough guys, I think. No snow today, but I can promise you, it has been another chiller. I'm not sure whether I'll ever get used to this. Where's that sunshine everybody keeps promising me? This weather is a nightmare. No matter how hard you try, it is impossible to get loose and even worse it is hard to have fun on a cricket field when you don't want the ball to come to you. I can't let anybody know that of course. Keep gutsing it out, mate.

Reading the paper this morning, I was quoted by a journalist as saying, 'One thing's for sure, this convict is going to make a shed full of runs this summer.' Never one for making big statements about my form, I was surprised to read this quote. I had talked to the journo, and maybe I do have a gut feeling that I will make plenty of runs this summer, but I definitely didn't call myself a convict. So the question reared its head, am I supposed to take offence at this? After the Ashes tour last summer, a few of the yobbos in the crowd suggested we 'take our balls and chains and go home to where we belong', and, even worse, 'that Aussies are only our throw-aways, the ones we didn't want'. Ouch. That hurt and I guess I could have got myself worked up about it, but what's the point? All friendly banter I decided. But now one thing's fair, if I settle for being a convict, and a very proud and patriotic one at that, you can't take offence at me calling you a 'pom' throughout this book. All friendly Aussie banter now! Fair's fair, you have a deal if we can agree on that. No offence meant, I promise.

Tuesday, 21 April – at least we tried

It is the chill factor which gets you. Sitting on the Canterbury balcony watching this morning's proceedings, I was clad in my normal attire for the week: T-shirt, sleeveless sweater, jacket, cricket trousers, two pairs of socks and a beanie hat for my freezing ears. It wasn't until Mark Ramprakash warned me that Kent may be planning to forfeit their first innings and I would be required to bat again that the chill factor really grabbed me.

Stepping into the changing-room with Middlesex

nine wickets down, I started to shiver – and shiver and shiver. Even when I replaced my jacket with a cricket shirt and long-sleeved sweater, I just kept shivering. I don't think it was the extra nerves of having to bat again but just the fact that the cold had grabbed me like a big cold bear hug. I understood what it must be like to be really cold – not ideal for playing cricket, that's for sure.

Just what I don't feel like. It's not that I don't want to bat, it's just that I feel as stiff as a frozen tree branch and in this weather I don't know how I'm going to get my feet dancing at the crease like I want them to. Come on, fire up you wimp. This is what you are here for, to make as many runs as possible.

Our last wicket did fall and, as predicted, Kent's captain Steve Marsh forfeited his team's first innings. We scored 22 runs in seven overs in order to set Kent 250 off sixty overs for an outright victory.

So this is what they mean by contrived results in county cricket!

Often this is the hardest time to bat, part-time bowlers tossing up full tosses, enticing the big shots and quick scoring. Although you never admit it, your pride and ego scares you to death worrying about getting out to one of these pie-throwers. My opening partner, Richard Kettleborough, must have said ten times on our way from the changing-room to the pitch, 'I will die if I get out to this shit.' I know what he meant, his thoughts sum up the feeling of the situation perfectly.

Luckily, we scored the runs without too much incident, although I must admit, one of Matthew Walker's 'nude' off-spinners (ie. totally without spin!) kept a little low and as I chopped down on it I could almost feel the ball hitting my pad, dead in front of the wickets. It is a funny feeling when something like that happens. For the next few deliveries you tend to watch the ball a little more closely than before to ensure there is no lonely walk back to the pavilion. The torment of losing your wicket to a part-timer is enough to leave you dragging your heels along the ground all the way back to your waiting team-mates, who make things even worse by laughing their bloody heads off.

Having avoided the tormenting laughter, the scene was set. Kent needed 250 off sixty overs on a drying wicket. Their task in my eyes was a very difficult one. Their batsmen had had little batting in match conditions due to the poor pre-season weather patterns, and our bowlers, led by Angus Fraser, were desperate to put their pre-season fitness to the test.

Kent's task looked even harder after their openers fell cheaply, but a partnership between Walker and seasoned professional Alan Wells turned the momentum back in favour of the home side. One thing in England, which I also noted last summer, is that a team chasing runs can quickly turn the rhythm of the game due to the flat wickets and lightning-fast outfields. Today was no different. Although we dropped a few chances, due mainly to our ice-tipped fingers, their batsmen played the situation perfectly and in the end cruised to a full-point victory. Wells, Walker and Matthew Fleming, who is an outstanding competitor and talented all-rounder, secured the game for Kent, who are desperate to make up for three bridesmaid second placings from last summer.

The result was disappointing for an energised Middlesex, but I feel we can be encouraged by our attitude of going all out for an outright victory. With this extraordinary weather, manufactured results, while frustrating, at least make for exciting cricket and that is why we play the game. Sure Kent took the points, but at least we gave ourselves a fighting chance of driving back to London with winners' smiles on our faces. It wasn't to be this time but with the attitude we showed here, I believe we will have a successful summer, if those black clouds and icy breezes go away.

CHAPTER TWO
Weather Permitting

[illegible]

Wednesday, 22 April – chaos on the airwaves

[illegible]

ing what it must feel like to be a breadcrumb in an ants nest, we eventually arrived home at about 9.30 [illegible]

The morning [illegible]

Wednesday, 22 April – chaos on the motorways

The rigours of English professional cricket and the frustrations of English traffic congestion today took its toll. Only one week into the season and I am quickly realising that I am in for a long summer.

What have I got myself into, the demon in my brain keeps asking.

Canterbury to West Hampstead last night should have been a breeze. It would have been for the more experienced campaigner. After getting terribly lost somewhere between Surrey and the West End, and understanding what it must feel like to be a breadcrumb in an ants' nest, we eventually arrived home at about 9.30 p.m. rather than the estimated and promised time of arrival – 'We should be back about seven or seven thirty, Babe.'

This morning I had a few hours to open a bank account, reintroduce myself to my wife and daughter and then leave for our journey up north to Lancashire.

What was supposed to be a quick trip on the M1 and M6 is a story in itself.

Before leaving, I agreed to drive down to Lord's to pick up a few things for Buck. From our flat in West Hampstead we are talking 2.1 miles to Lord's; a perfect location and very convenient for my home ground. A bit wet behind the ears in terms of London traffic, I figured a 4.2-mile round trip should take me five or ten minutes, shouldn't it? Fifty minutes later I arrived back at the flat shaking my head but laughing at the absurdity of the situation. Fifty minutes! Admittedly I missed the St John's Wood turn-off from Abbey Road and had to fluke a three-point turn in the middle of 3.30 p.m. London traffic, but surely that is a long time to travel four miles to get from A to B and back?

This was only the start of my nightmare afternoon in the car. That initial fifty-minute trip immediately put Buck and me behind time. A team meeting was scheduled for 7.00 p.m. in Lancashire and considering we were now leaving home at 4.00 p.m. instead of 3.00 p.m., we were always going to be in trouble. This was magnified when we took the wrong turn-off from the North Circular road in London and had to drive six miles in the opposite direction before we could find a U-turn back towards the M1. After this thirty-minute mistake, we eventually found ourselves flying up the M1 towards Nottingham and Leicester, but this suddenly turned into a snail-paced crawl as we turned on to the M6 for Birmingham.

The traffic master device in my borrowed Vauxhall had warned us of the delay: 'You are travelling northbound towards junction seven. Very slow traffic. Expect a thirty-minute delay.' As the traffic packed further and further back up the motorway the female computer voice continued to preach disastrous news. 'Very slow traffic' was replaced by 'Traffic is at a standstill. Avoid at all costs if possible. Expect a seventy-minute delay.'

For the life of me I cannot work out how this traffic master is so accurate. It is a very clever and worthwhile device but also one which could find itself ripped out of my car and thrown into one of the rape-seed fields as a result of sheer frustration by the end of the summer. This voice so tranquil and relieving when the traffic is flowing freely turns into a voice from a horror movie when the traffic is running against you.

In one hour we travelled six miles between junctions seven and ten through Birmingham. To add to this frustration, heavy rain and angry black clouds hovered dauntingly in the exact direction we were heading. More rain meant more days sitting in the changing-room staring at the blue plastic covers, reduced to practising in the indoor nets and drinking cups of hot tea. Perhaps the rain would miss Lancashire but somehow even my most optimistic mind had grave doubts!

Eventually the traffic freed up and we were back in positive action again; that was until we took the wrong M56 turn-off and found ourselves driving towards North Wales. That definitely didn't sound right. As I know from experience, North Wales isn't really that close to Cheadle in Manchester.

Oh well, what was one more wrong turn for the day. The digital clock had already ticked over to 7.45 p.m. What was an extra fifteen minutes' delay when we were already forty-five minutes late for the team meeting and dinner? At least I was with the coach so I couldn't get into too much trouble. While we both knew we would be fined, or at least given a hard time by our team-mates, our argument was that Angus Fraser, the transport manager, should take all the blame for putting two backward Aussies together in a land of mysterious motorways and signpostings.

Surprisingly, our case worked and we were forgiven for our first misdemeanour of the summer. We may have escaped being fined, but stiff backs, frustrated, jaded brains and a truckload of insults from our mates made up for anything a fine could have achieved. Five hours in a car was punishment enough for our ill-prepared performance on the road. The traffic jams Buck and I are used to are more like a drive in the country on a sunny Sunday afternoon; we had already paid the price.

Eventually we had a late team meeting, but as the rain battered the windows outside, we all had the feeling that our preparation could be in vain.

Thursday, 23 April – where are my wellies?

Our team meeting may well have been in vain. We arrived at Old Trafford to find a ground resembling a Christmas rugby pitch rather than a firm county cricket ground. Every step from the pavilion to the centre square was a squelching affair, and my new Kookaburra boots could have been appropriately exchanged for a pair of Wellington boots.

While the wicket looks well grassed and reasonably dry, it was no surprise that the umpires called off the day's proceedings after lunch, due to the waterlogged outfield. The one big bonus in this is that the Lancashire pro and beneficiary, one Wasim Akram, will have less of a chance to rocket a ball into my ribs or flick my backside with one of his swinging or seaming thunderbolts. A new cricket ball in his hand is always one of the great challenges facing any first-class batsman.

A brief reprieve from Wasim is about the only positive I can muster from yet another cricketless day spent watching the rain fall at Old Trafford. The time in the changing-room at least rekindles very fond memories of last season when Steve Waugh wrote his name, yet again, into the record books. His centuries in both innings of the third Test proved major catalysts in the victory that evened up the Ashes series, one all. The last time I walked out of the Old Trafford changing-rooms I was in a far less sober state than I was today. In fact, the visitors' rooms have been refurbished and are first class. After the beer and champagne saturation they received following that Test victory, it is hardly surprising to see that they have been renovated.

What a party we had in those tired old rooms; talk about enjoying a victory. After being trounced in the one-day series and then the first Test at Edgbaston, it was a huge relief for the guys finally to have a win and regain some pride. In true Aussie style the celebration which followed further increased the spirit and atmosphere in the team, which helped us go from strength to strength in the series. Retaining the Ashes was a product of this renewed team spirit, an aspect so vital in any successful team.

Friday, 24 April – rain, rain, go away!

What worries me is the number of people starting to comment about the weather. 'I haven't seen this wet a start to the cricket season for years. I can't remember the last April like this,' they say. Then before I even have a chance to acknowledge the comment, they start getting defensive about it. 'It isn't always this wet, you know.' It is a bad sign when everyone starts talking about the weather. It is tough enough surviving the constant rain let alone listening to how it usually is. Even worse is the comment I must have heard one thousand times since I arrived in the UK: 'January and February were so mild, they were beautiful months. I can't understand this change.'

Yeah, Yeah! Don't tell me that, I couldn't care less how good it was three months ago. Save me the dramatics, please. Why don't you just admit you have shitty weather here in England?

I just keep smiling and accepting the sympathetic observations. There is no point arguing about the facts and, more importantly, there is absolutely nothing we can do about the weather except hope it will improve. It has to, doesn't it? It can't get any worse!

My heart sympathises with the flood-stricken countries of China and Bangladesh. This is nothing compared with those tragic places. We might be missing a few days of cricket, that's all. Put it in perspective, you goose!

* * *

Day two was called off before lunch; a little premature considering the sky was clear and blue all afternoon. Admittedly the ground at Old Trafford is still very wet and muddy, almost like a swampy plain, so I guess the umpires saved us the boredom of another changing-room farce.

One benefit of yet another abandoned day was the opportunity to practise in the Old Trafford Indoor Centre. This facility is nothing short of world class and I would say it must be close to the most impressive indoor facility I have seen anywhere around the world. Not only is it huge, but its surface is excellent for practice. They tell me the England side spent a week here before travelling to the West Indies in the winter. Hardly a surprise seeing how good the facility really is.

Buck had the guys in the nets for a two-hour session followed by an hour of fielding drills in the indoor centre. By the scheduled lunch-break at 12.15 p.m., we had really earned our tucker. I get the feeling this new intensive training schedule being introduced by the rookie county coach is surprising a few of the guys. By the sounds of things, the boys normally would have been back at the hotel relaxing as soon as the umpires had made their decision on the state of the day's play.

The approach of training hard and preparing thoroughly for a game, so normal to me, seems foreign to many of the squad. I must admit, though, the majority of the guys are grasping the new format really well. I am sure everyone at Middlesex is going to reap the rewards of the John Buchanan style of coaching. No stone will be left unturned, and from what I am seeing first hand, and hearing from the Queensland cricketers, who Buck coaches in Australia, each player will be given a great opportunity to improve every facet of his game under Buck's enthusiastic guidance.

The hard work being done is sure to have a positive effect as the season unfolds. Let's hope so anyway! Surely it has to be better than sitting in your hotel room drinking tea and dunking your biscuits.

Saturday, 25 April – play at last!

A bird chirping! Could that be a good sign? First one eye opened in anxious anticipation, then my second eye a little quicker as I sensed a ray of sunshine hiding behind the heavy curtains of my hotel room. Jumping out of bed it was almost a sprint to go and see, the spring in my step encouraged by the prospect of blue sky and cloudlessness. Could we actually be on the park today? If the 7.00 a.m. skies were anything to go by we were looking good.

Amazingly, play started on time and although Ramps lost the toss for the third time running, it was great to get out into the middle. Even if the pitch looked like it might offer some assistance to the bowlers, anything was better than indoor practice and sitting on your backside in the changing-room.

Batting at Old Trafford took a little getting used to as the pitch was very slow, and although Akram didn't play, the Lancashire attack was spirited and lively. By tea, my team-mates had batted with discipline to be 205 for 4 with young gun Owais Shah on 64 and Paul Weekes on 20.

'Ace' Shah, the captain of the Under-19s who won

the Junior World Cup in South Africa, has had a great press since I arrived and if today is anything to go by, he looks a true talent for the future. I look forward to watching his progress throughout the season.

At tea, as has become commonplace in this wettest April for many years, a rain cloud the size of the Grand Canyon and as black and heavy as a chain smoker's lung made its way over Old Trafford. Optimistically, and foolishly, we hoped it would go around us but the reality was a Niagara Falls downpour, which dashed hopes of any more play today, and perhaps hopes of play on Sunday and Monday. The ground, as waterlogged as it is, is almost begging for mercy from the water gods above. 'It just can't take any more,' was the cry from the old Lancashire supporter in the crowd, who looked like part of the Old Trafford furniture. We must wait and see.

The added frustration is the amount of play around the country. Old Trafford is the only ground where the game is not progressing and thus the other counties are potentially accumulating early season points, which could be vital come the end of the season.

Sunday, 26 April – marking time with 'Tuffers'

The big brother of yesterday's almighty rain cloud decided to pay us a visit today. He had the same damning effect, wiping out the second Sunday League fixture of the season.

A brilliant gymnasium at the hotel helped to keep us in shape and blow out the frustrations of cricketlessness. Although this extra work in the nets and gym won't do us any harm, I can sense the guys want to get out and start playing cricket. You can't make any runs or take any wickets in the nets. Trying hard to remain cheerful, the restlessness may have a positive effect on the way we all play our cricket.

A hungry lion is always the best hunter.

Cricket tomorrow? I can't see it. Not in Lancashire anyway.

I'm starting to feel a little guilty. I'm being paid a handsome salary for little return at present, but there is absolutely nothing I can do about this precipitation. There will be plenty of time to earn my keep I'm sure.

With the chance of play tomorrow unlikely, I was lucky to spend a few hours in the bar with Phil Tufnell. What an experience! I get the feeling he and I could be pretty good mates by the end of the summer. Talk about laugh! Most of the evening was spent wiping the tears from my eyes as Tuffers recounted a few of the more eventful incidents in his life.

A night with Tuffers is not unlike spending a night with Merv Hughes. The laughs are endless. With his strong cockney accent and a few pints of lager under his belt the man is hilarious. In between fags, England's most talented spinner (in my opinion) swings his arms around like an Italian politician as he gets right into every detail of his stories. Classic entertainment!

I have already offered to be his agent in setting up speaking engagements around the country. If you read about me retiring from cricket to become a sports promoter, you will know what I am doing. Nonetheless, if you ever see an advertisement inviting you to 'Spend a Night with Tuffers', I can promise you it will be a night to remember. Amazingly, he feels shy in front of an audience, so his career as an after-dinner speaker may not get off the blocks, but hopefully he will keep working on it.

Tuffers was telling me about the Sunday morning when he walked down to the corner shop to buy a paper. Shock, horror and disbelief grabbed him by the heart when he picked up the paper to see the headline 'Test Cricketer's Wife on the Game'. As he described his dismay at his ex-wife's apparent behaviour after the divorce, you could see in his face and hear by the tone of his voice that he still didn't know whether to laugh or cry. I almost got the impression that Tuffers had the feeling that 'it could only happen to me'.

Obviously being the high-profile player that he is in England, his much-publicised scrapes with the authorities, whether they be team management or police officers, are sure to make the news. It is both interesting and very funny to hear Tuffers' side of the story. He had me in stitches recalling what really happened. By the sounds of it, the news reports are almost always about one tenth of the real story. That's what Tuffers told me anyway!

Lying in bed, my guts feel like I have just done a thousand sit-ups from the last three hours of laughter.

Of the games played today, the big news hitting Ceefax was the second century of the match for newly appointed Sussex captain, Chris Adams. After leaving Derbyshire during the winter for a reportedly huge sum of money, the media pressure has been building. This outstanding match performance today is the best possible answer. Having played him at Derbyshire last summer, I remember him as one of the sweetest and cleanest hitters of the cricket ball I have seen. He is a very good player and I hope he will be having an off day on Wednesday when we play him in the first round of the Benson & Hedges Cup at Lord's. Reports are that he could be pushing hard for an England debut in the international one-day series coming up. We will have to ask England selector Mike Gatting tomorrow while we watch the rain fall.

Monday, 27 April – unwise diversion

Play didn't even look like getting started at Old Trafford today. The only cricket played was yet another long training session before the boys headed back up the motorway for London. Buck and I should have learnt from our mistakes on the way to Lancashire five days ago. The advice given was, 'Don't be passing through Birmingham between 3.00 and 6.00 p.m. as there are regular traffic delays daily around that period.'

Unfortunately, the 'she'll be right, mate' option didn't work for us yet again. We figured that being in Manchester was too good an opportunity to miss out on visiting Manchester United Football Club. Even though we had four days to visit, we decided to leave it to the last minute.

Good thinking, idiots!

* * *

What a set-up at this incredible club! The ground is awesome with a nine-year waiting list for the corporate boxes. One of the grandstands, with the capacity to hold a sell-out crowd at Lord's, is very similar to the Great Southern Stand in Melbourne, although the smaller arena makes it look even vaster. The breathtaking feeling as you walk into the MCG for the first time is the same as the one you get when you step into the Old Trafford football stadium.

The tour given to us by Fred, the Manchester United guide, was enthralling and exciting, but the novelty soon wore off as we sat in a six-mile traffic jam between junctions five and eight through Birmingham. The traffic master had warned us, the locals had warned us, even the radio had warned us. How dumb are we? Surely we will know better next time?

By 7.30 p.m. we were back in London, carrying bags of souvenirs from the Manchester United megastore but disappointed at having played only two sessions of cricket in five days. What a week it has been!

Tuesday, 28 April – Daddy's home

A day off, wow! Even though we haven't been playing all that much cricket, it is nice to spend a day away from the cricket environment when the opportunity presents itself. Morning warm-ups, changing-rooms and the same male faces are all part of the job, but it is terrific to spend time with your wife and daughter every now and then.

Apart from family re-uniting, the day was spent meeting with the management at Middlesex, finalising my contract and making sure everything is in order for the season. It just goes to show how tight the English county schedule really is. I have been in the country for two weeks and today is the first day I have had available to sort out my county contract.

The next two weeks are less intense with a number of one-day fixtures on the cards. After this round of one-dayers, we are back into the intensive and energy-consuming programme of county cricket. It will be interesting to see how the players keep going for the whole season. I guess it will be the players who are most hungry for success who will stand out and maintain the necessary level of motivation.

I spoke on the phone to the Worcestershire skipper Tom Moody tonight. He has played English county cricket for ten seasons; he asked me how I was settling in and how I was enjoying myself. In my enthusiasm, I said I was having a great time, my team-mates and the club were brilliant and I thought the lifestyle of county cricket was sensational. Cricket every day, what could be better? He listened and finished the conversation with a few words of wisdom.

'Yeah mate, it is a pretty good lifestyle, but just wait until you start playing cricket every single day and your body and mind start crying out for a bit of a break. We'll see how much you are enjoying yourself then. It is pretty hard work, just hang in there.'

Coming from 'Moods', who is the most durable and seasoned cricket campaigner I know, these words could be something of an ominous warning. So far so good for me, but I suspect that every day off could become more and more enticing as the season progresses.

Wednesday, 29 April – Lord's at last!

There was method in Middlesex's decision to have me open the batting for the county. Scoring a mountain of runs throughout the season was their main objective in signing me, but on this occasion they had the forethought to provide me with an opening partner to help me find my way through the Lord's Long Room and onto the hallowed turf of cricket's Mecca. With my poor record for getting lost and losing my sense of direction, it would have been insane, and totally unfair, for the Middlesex hierarchy to send me out to the Lord's pitch all alone. Imagine turning up this morning to play my first home game for my adopted club only to get myself timed out simply because I couldn't find my way from the home dressing-room to the pitch. Considering my recent form with getting from A to B, this would have been a distinct possibility. Thankfully, Keith Brown, my one-day opening partner, was there to guide me and I successfully made it to the Lord's crease in a Middlesex cap for the first time.

It is quite a daunting journey through the Lord's Long Room, a room saturated with the rich history of our wonderful game. Dressed in my new Middlesex sweater and helmet, it was nerve-racking passing by the portraits of Hutton, Grace and Bradman, all of whom seem to blend in with the very much alive Middlesex and MCC members watching me go on my way. I wonder, as these distinguished-looking gentlemen politely wish me luck with a smile and a nod, what they are thinking to themselves as I pass them by. Probably something along the lines of 'Who is this little Aussie pro we have signed up this year? I hope he is a good'un. We will be looking for plenty of runs from him this season. He better not let us down.' This pressure of expectation multiplies my anxiety to make an impression, and I haven't even faced a ball yet.

Standing at the non-striker's end, waiting for the first ball of the match to be delivered, I can't help but think to myself, 'Things can't get much better than this.' My home ground is the Mecca of cricket; I am standing at the wicket on a beautiful blue English morning, favourite bat in hand, the magnificent Lord's grandpa pavilion as the backdrop and none other than Dickie Bird adjudicating from my end; the pitch looks good, the boundary short on one side and Mr Bird, a cricketing icon, has smiled at me, wished me a good morning and good luck and told me, before I can speak, that this is his last season umpiring and he is intending to enjoy himself. How good is this? Nothing could stop me from enjoying this monumental occasion.

Now watch the bloody ball like a hawk. This is very nice enjoying the occasion but unless you watch that ball, you'll be back in the pavilion feeling sorry for yourself. You can't make any runs watching from the sidelines. Come on, watch that ball . . . shit.

Nothing except an inswinger from the Sussex opening bowler which came back down the slope and cleaned up my stumps before I could really trouble the scorers – out for three in my debut innings at home for Middlesex. The walk back is always hard, but walking back with the grandpa pavilion frowning down on you makes it even harder.

* * *

This'll be good. I wonder what the old fellas in their suits are going to think of me now.

You reckon walking through the Long Room on the way out to the crease is bad. Try doing it after you have just failed. There is no escape; you have to walk back past those now silent members, in their jackets and gold and orange ties, who seem to be judging your every move. They say first impressions mean the world. I hope this isn't the case here. I will have to make up for it next innings.

The game progressed and Middlesex scored 283 from our allocated fifty overs. Keith Brown scored a brilliant century. If Alec Stewart is elected captain of England later this week, the selectors may be looking for a replacement keeper. Surely there is no way anyone could expect Stewart to open the batting, keep wicket and captain the side? He is not superman. The rumour I am hearing is that 'Browny' may have an outside chance of selection. England could do worse than have a player with the fighting instincts of this character keeping wicket and batting down the order. Performances like today's can do him no harm.

Good contributions came from all our players, especially a revitalised Paul Weekes who hits the ball as sweet as candy. His 68 not out guided the team to our massive score.

One-day cricket is never over until the last ball is bowled, as was the case today. Chris Adams continued his supreme form smashing 54 off fewer balls. He hit one almighty six off Gus Fraser, which rocketed into the Long Room window – a shot of which even the great Vivian Richards would have been proud. The game came down to Sussex needing 12 runs off the last over. A six was hit off the second ball from 'Weekesy'. With tensions mounting, our off-spinner produced four great deliveries leaving us victors by five runs. Winning, like losing, is a habit and I am hopeful this first victory of the season is going to start things off for the team.

From all accounts, today is the first Benson & Hedges Cup victory over a first-class county for Middlesex in three seasons. It is a positive start, even if I didn't make the contribution I would have liked. Today really has been a day to remember. I love my new home ground.

Thursday, 30 April – Lord's, oh lovely Lord's!

Looking back on yesterday, I can't help thinking about the awesome atmosphere created by just being at Lord's. Everything about the place makes you excited at playing a game of cricket. Leaving home yesterday morning was, for me, similar to the feeling I used to get as a kid when I woke up on Christmas morning and ran in to the lounge room to open my bag of presents.

Getting into the car and working my way through the Finchley traffic was, for once, no chore, as I knew that within fifteen minutes I would be arriving at the international home of cricket and unpacking my bags ready for the day ahead. Just being there is a day out in itself, let alone being lucky enough to play cricket there for a living.

The home changing-room is massive, with all the luxuries of being in your own home. There is nothing worse than turning up to a venue where the dressing-rooms are small and cold, with concrete floors and wooden benches, and where cricket bags, smelly team-mates, a physio bench and a first-aid kit are crammed in on top of each other like sardines crammed into their claustrophobic metal tin.

Lord's does not conform to this normal description of a cricket changing-room. It provides carpeted floors, central heating, cushioned benches, space, space and more space, hot tea and coffee, and food of all descriptions to keep you going through the day. This is certainly the life; the only danger is the temptation of spending more time in here than out on the park sweating it out scoring runs, taking wickets or pulling off unlikely catches.

Even the showers are something else. I remember leaving Lord's after the one-day international last summer, in awe of these fantastic shower-heads. You may think I am crazy, but you have to see them to know what I am talking about. There is nothing like a long, hot shower after six and a half hours on a cricket field and you can be sure to get one of these when you play a game of cricket at Lord's. It is like standing under a hot steamy waterfall, such is the size of these shower-heads; huge, stainless steel heads the size of dinner plates, pouring steaming water out like a Mercedes car wash. Simply fantastic!

If you have had a really good, or long, day in the field and you feel like treating yourself to an equally long, hot bath, then, surprise, surprise, Lord's can even offer you one of these. The old baths are as big as an Olympic swimming pool and although they may take a while to fill up, the pleasure is well worth the wait.

To top off the showers and baths, you have the most amazing lunch menu of all time. After a main course of the highest quality hot food, you can look forward to the most delicious choice of puddings imaginable. Hot treacle pudding, apple pie, spotted dick, chocolate pudding, the list goes on. I am convinced the chef at Lord's has been headhunted from one of the top London restaurants.

It sounds like I have been advertising a first-class hotel by the way I have described the facilities. Throw in one of the most beautifully kept backyards in the world, wonderful paintings, shops, indoor training facilities, a museum and a media centre of world-class standard and you can understand why a day playing at Lord's is an experience in itself.

Obviously, the hazards of a men's changing-room remain. In one corner, David Nash's crusty, dirty jock-straps lie around like a lioness about to pounce on its unsuspecting prey, and Tim Bloomfield's used socks, which smell like an old fishing shed, are enough to make even the strongest stomach squirm. On the balcony side of the room, Tuffers' and Keith Dutch's fag smoke drifts in and out like the thick mist of the English Channel. It is never unusual to have clouds of smoke in a changing-room; although sickening, it adds an aroma so common in a nervous team occupancy. And to top it all off, Gatt often walks around in his birthday suit showing off his pimply backside to anyone unfortunate enough to get in its way; not the sort of sight you would like to see with a Sunday morning hangover.

These regular hazards aside, how lucky do you think this Aussie left-hander feels to have been adopted by the club with the greatest facilities in the world? My only problem will be ensuring the hot puddings don't leave me looking as though I have swallowed a sheep by the end of this English summer.

Friday, 1 May – stick to cricket

The train system in London is brilliant. Within half an hour I had arrived in the south-west of London. Had I taken the uneducated option and attempted to drive from West Hampstead to Richmond at 8 a.m. this morning, I would have more than likely still been driving at midday. A Middlesex sponsors' golf day had me teeing off at 9.00 a.m., so challenging the London traffic in the car was hardly high on my priority list, unless of course I left home before the sun came up.

Sticky buns and coffee in the lovely warm clubhouse were almost ruined by the call of tee-off time. Surprise, surprise, as I swung the golf club on the first tee I felt like the tin man from *The Wizard of Oz*. Everyone from the weatherman on TV to Joe Bloggs on the street promises me that the weather will get better, but I must admit I am starting to question these expert judgements as every day passes. So cold was I today playing golf, my trousers felt like they had frozen solid and my nose and ears, even covered by my Middlesex beanie hat, felt as though they would snap off like a mass of frozen peas. Even my best friend the pocket handwarmer could do little to help me feel the slightest bit comfortable as I trudged around the beautiful, but frosty, Royal Mid Surrey golf course.

The fact that the sponsors thrashed Keith Brown and myself helped top off a pretty miserable day; my golf was so bad you would have thought I was playing left-handed just for fun. I can't remember hitting one ball in the middle.

Give up, son, stick to cricket. You're kidding yourself.

We always hear about 'whingeing poms' in Australia; well, I will be the first to admit I can understand what they may be whingeing about when they experience the extreme heat while visiting Australia. This cold for me is unbelievable; it leaves you feeling stiff and sorry. I don't know how the Eskimos do it.

Fortunately Denise Fraser, Angus's wife, cooked us a magnificent meal tonight. This fine food, a couple of bottles of Australian red wine and excellent company, in our physio Simon Shephard, his wife Tracy, Buck and Alistair Fraser, a one-day specialist for Middlesex and younger brother of Angus, helped to salvage my sanity for the day. That is until my daughter tore the wallpaper off the Frasers' newly decorated walls. How embarrassing! There we are eating a lovely dinner, trying to make new friends in a foreign land, while in the living room, sweet and innocent little Jessica is entertaining herself by tearing strips of wallpaper from our hosts' walls. What a little monster! Halfway through my seafood lasagne, Jess came toddling into the dining room, eyes staring at the floor, holding a handful of floral wallpaper. The horror and embarrassment of it all was too much to bear as the realisation of her little party trick dawned upon Sue and me.

The problem is what do you do when something like this happens? Jump up and down, rant and rave like lunatic parents? Smile and apologise and hope everyone understands that she has never done anything like this before? There is no simple solution. We settled for a couple more bottles of wine to calm the nerves of our hosts, a severe reprimand for the villain and a sincere 'sucking up' approach, maybe for the rest of the summer. Fortunately, the Frasers remain friends, I think. As we left, they didn't say let's do this again. I wonder why?

Hanging on the walls of the Fraser household are a number of paintings by Jack Russell. He is a talented artist who combines his artistic prowess and professional cricket very well. I might have to purchase some of his work while I am in England; his paintings are excellent depictions of cricket scenes around the world. Lucky they were out of Jessica's reach or she may have pulled them down as well.

CHAPTER THREE
The One-Day Whirlwind

Saturday, 2 May – one-day cricket

Training this morning at Lord's was long and intense in preparation for the next week of one-day cricket. Five one-day games in nine days will help decide if we make the quarter-finals of the Benson & Hedges Cup and give us an opportunity to add to our Sunday League standing. It is incredible that the equivalent of a whole season of Australian domestic one-day cricket will be played within a total of nine days in this country.

Our domestic one-day competition, the Mercantile Mutual Cup, consists of five one-day fixtures, followed by the semi-finals and final if your team is lucky enough to progress. In contrast, the English system constitutes seventeen forty-over games, four fifty-over B&H Cup games plus quarter-finals, semi-finals and final, and a sixty-over NatWest Cup one-day competition. In reality, English cricketers play at least five times more one-day cricket in a season than we do in Australia.

While there has been heated discussion about the shape of English cricket, I know that the Australian Cricket Board is currently in the middle of an extensive overview of the Australian system. One of the issues is whether we play enough one-day cricket in our domestic season. The general consensus between the players and, I believe, the administrators, is that we need more one-day cricket in our itinerary. A case is being put forward to have the states play each other twice each season rather than once. With the increase in international one-day cricket and the 1999 World Cup, it seems more may be better in the domestic Australian summer. How it works, and the logistics of such a change, must be settled by the administrators of the game as we go into the twenty-first century.

The big question is, does more cricket make for better cricket? I guess the results of the World Cup in 1999 will help judge that. On one hand, you may argue an increase in one-day fixtures will help players develop new skills and learn the best techniques of mastering the one-day game. If this is the case, England should consistently prove to be the world leaders in the shorter version of the game. No other country plays the sheer weight of games that English county players have the opportunity to play in. This in mind, it would be simple to figure that English players should be the most experienced and skilled one-day players in the world. The problem I see for England is that although they play a lot of one-dayers, the quality of all their games may be in danger of deteriorating rather than constantly improving, simply because of the demands placed on the players. As players become wearier with the daily requirements of the sport, the quality of the game is in danger of becoming less intense and less cutthroat with every encounter of the summer.

The smart county player could view his itinerary for the season with excited anticipation because of the vast opportunities to improve his game and push for personal improvement. Unfortunately, I am already sensing that a large number of county players see one-day games as just another day at the office, just another game of cricket.

In contrast, the limited exposure in the Australian domestic one-day set-up promotes intense competition between the states, but provides less opportunity for players to develop their skills and show off their talents to the Australian selectors. It is for this reason that I am so stimulated about playing county cricket. I will have the opportunity to squeeze five seasons of one-dayers into one, a buzz for me as I know that one-day cricket is an area where I can improve.

The trend in world cricket is for an increase in the limited-overs game. The public, and therefore the sponsors, want more one-day cricket so the administrators are doing everything possible to satisfy the demand. Most players are happy to play more games, not only because we enjoy wearing coloured clothing and hitting more sixes but also because of the generally larger crowds and added financial incentives involved.

In my opinion, the administrators should strive for an even balance – the public should get what they want in more pyjama cricket, but at the same time care must be taken not to over-saturate the demand. It is also important that the players don't lose their appetite for the game by playing too much. I am sure the public isn't attracted only by the glamour and assured result of a one-day game but also by the prospect of seeing fit, athletic players entertaining with brilliant fielding, fast running between the wickets and aggressive batting. The only way this will be jeopardised in today's professional market is if the participants lose their physical fitness and desire to perform at the highest possible level day in, day out – a danger, if they are put on a conveyor belt that doesn't have a stop, or at least a rest and prepare, button sitting on its control panel.

Sunday, 3 May – victory celebrations

Something confuses me about English cricket – the lack of joy and celebration from the players after a victory. In my eyes, it is typical of the conveyor belt phenomenon – with so many matches played, even a victory is just another game. Win, lose or draw, it doesn't seem to make all that much difference to the players. Obviously the boys would prefer to win – we all like to win – but however it finishes we all know that we will be back doing it again tomorrow and the next day and the next. A win to an English player seems to be similar to a stockbroker having an up day with his equities, and conversely a loss or draw is nothing more than a down day in the market.

Today Middlesex enjoyed a sensational victory over Glamorgan at Lord's in the Sunday League. In reality, we really snatched a victory from the jaws of defeat, showing once again the value of batting out your full allocation of overs in limited-overs cricket. Fast bowler Richard Johnson's massive six over cover, from nothing less than a Waqar Younis thunderbolt, turned the impetus back in our favour with only three overs remaining. Considering we were in trouble at 80 for 5, chasing 218, the victory to me was very encouraging; it not only highlighted the fighting qualities of a young team, but it also extended our winning streak from one game to two. Not bad, taking into account Middlesex's lack of success in one-day cricket in the last few seasons.

Disappointingly, a heartening win was followed by a few moments of backslapping and handshaking, and within ten minutes half of the team had left the rooms for the day. Now it is only a minor gripe because the fact is we had won the game, earned the points and enjoyed a great day, but in my eyes, victory is a time for celebration and revelry. In sport, and for that matter, in life, there is a high proportion of time spent at the down or mundane end of the scale, so it is important to celebrate and enjoy the high times. Isn't it?

Last summer, I can recall visiting the England changing-room after a couple of their one-day and Test victories. To my surprise, I found the rooms half empty and far from a state of winning euphoria as I would have expected. Most of the players didn't have time to sit around and enjoy a victory celebration, as they had to get back on to the motorway for a county game the next day.

If more emphasis was placed on each game played, the conveyor belt may stop for a brief moment, enabling the players to express the joy of success and reflect upon a job well done! It is sad to see a lot of people acting as though county cricket is nothing more than a job. It makes it hard to see every game as an event, something that I am so used to where I come from. Here, the guys turn up in shirt and tie every morning and by ten minutes after stumps they are generally showered, dressed and packed up for the day. Unless the attitude changes, it will be difficult to nurture the county circuit as a solid stepping-stone to Test cricket. If nothing else, it would be delightful to see my team-mates really enjoying the emotions of victory and getting more out of the game than just a pay cheque at the end of the month.

Here's to celebrating great victories like today's! Cheers!

Monday, 4 May – crazy Frenchmen!

Training at Lord's this morning was another long session. Buck has the squad working hard and although the guys are putting in the hard yards, I get the feeling they are enjoying the workload. It's astounding the fresh energy and exuberance generated from a couple of victories.

A day out was had by my Australian counterparts in the B&H Cup today. Darren Lehmann, who is playing for Yorkshire, and Worcestershire skipper Tom Moody took the man of the match awards in their respective games, while one-day genius Michael Bevan scored 95 not out for Sussex.

In my eyes, 'Bevo' has to be rated the number one short-game batsman in the world. A player averaging over 50 in international one-day cricket, who consistently plays a major part in a team's victory, is as valuable to his team as spinach is to Popeye. He could prove a very worthwhile signing for his new county club.

With no match on this bank holiday Monday, I was lucky to attend a lunch with three living legends from a different code. Michael Lynagh, François Pienaar and Philippe Sella, international rugby superstars and London Saracens imports, were invited guests at a lunch hosted by my good friend Nigel Wray. The Australian and Frenchman of the trio are gearing up for the final two games of their distinguished rugby careers. Both will retire at the end of this season, hopefully having taken out the England rugby double for 1998. It was a privilege lunching with such high achievers and gentlemen who play a crazy game like they do. These guys aren't that big. How they run and tackle their monstrous opponents is one of the marvels of the universe, if you ask me.

Philippe Sella found it hard to believe, when he first went to a cricket match, that the players actually left the field in the afternoon to have a cup of tea and a couple of scones with strawberry jam and whipped cream.

'What sort of game is this that you cricketers play?' he asked with a shake of the head and an honest, disbelieving smile. 'Too slow for me,' he went on, 'not enough action, and cups of tea in the middle. You people must be a little crazy.'

Fair call, I admitted, but anyone who stands less than six feet from the ground and runs around on freezing cold winters' afternoons in small, silky shorts, tackling monsters like Jonah Lomu for a living – well, who is the crazy one, I ask.

By the end of lunch we had decided to agree to differ on which game was the better one. In the end, I was just happy to have shared an excellent day with interesting company, eating fine food in one of the Italian restaurants in Hampstead.

Tuesday, 5 May – a childhood dream realised

Alec Stewart, the superman of English cricket, today stood proudly posing for the cricket paparazzi, chest out and showing off a smile as big as Buckingham Palace. Standing in the Mound Stand, overlooking the lush lawns of the Mecca of cricket, all Alec needed to top off his morning was the national anthem booming in the background. Playing for your country is one thing, leading it is another; an honour reserved for a few chosen men.

The press hadn't gathered in their droves to report on the progress of our B&H clash with Ireland at Lord's. As Angus Fraser stormed in from the Pavilion End to deliver his first ball to Ireland's opening batsman, Paddy McCrum, the press's attentions were firmly directed towards Alec Stewart and his plans for the future of English cricket. Amid all the questions and photo flashes stood a man beaming like a proud new father, honoured by the promotion but, I am sure, wary of the challenges facing one of the world's most daunting positions. With all the perks of the job comes the equivalent pressure to that heaped upon the US President. His every move will be monitored, and the same English press, so friendly today, will be watching his performance like a hyena eyes a dying animal. Remarkably, the England selectors will ask 'Stewie' to continue wicketkeeping and yet again drop down the order from his preferred opening position. If captaining the side isn't enough, the expectation on him to perform three intense tasks is a massive one. By the end of the Test series, I wouldn't be surprised to see Superman Stewart back opening and captaining the side without the added pressure of playing the drummer in the band behind the stumps. As an Australian onlooker, it is surprising that Alec doesn't open the batting all the time. His game is perfectly suited to the opening role, as he plays the fast bowlers as well as any player in the game. Doing three jobs is tough, but if I was the sole selector of the England cricket team I would want to have him opening the batting for me every time, even if it means sacrificing the gloves.

Alec won't be the only proud Englishman walking with his head in the clouds today. The selectors also announced that Adam Hollioake will captain the England one-day side. This is a little surprising to me. I've nothing at all against Adam or his captaincy prowess; it just seems strange to appoint your Test captain, who happens to be your first choice in the one-day side, and yet not appoint him across the board in all forms of the game. It seems to take away the polish of the job, and potentially endangers the continuity, so important to moulding a successful team. When Mike Atherton's captaincy came to an end, it seemed to be a perfect opportunity for a fresh start for English cricket at the highest level. The selectors in their wisdom have decided to go with two separate leaders, a strange decision but one obviously made for a specific reason. Whether it is the right one will soon become apparent.

Australia has two captains, but only because the selectors don't believe Mark Taylor should be in the one-day first eleven. In recent times, Mark Taylor has expressed his belief that there should be only one captain rather than a separate leader for each game. I agree with Mark Taylor's belief in a one-captain set-up, hence my surprise at the latest English selection.

The trend is for two separate teams with specialist players being selected for the increasing number of one-day internationals. This is becoming accepted among the players but ideally I believe one captain is the best way to go. Maybe I should have asked Gatt about the England selectors' way of thinking when I was standing in the slips with him today; after all, he is one of them. It would have made for an interesting discussion, as we took out our third successive victory, against Ireland.

Thursday, 7 May – so that's what they think

Round three of the Benson & Hedges Cup gave us the opportunity to play at lovely Chelmsford, and take on Essex's adopted and favourite sons, Stuart Law and England vice-captain Nasser Hussain. On another freezing cold day, Middlesex fought back from two daunting situations to take the points and pave a secure path to the quarter-finals in a few weeks' time. Four victories straight and the pundits are reaching for the record books after a bare one-day cupboard in the last few seasons.

Last night's team meeting was more interesting than most for me. As part of the normal routine, we discussed the Essex batsmen. High on our assassination list was the name Stuart Law. Not only is he one of the most destructive players in county cricket, but his standing as a one-day player is respected internationally. My teammates plotted his downfall, but I was most interested in what Buck had to say about how we should attack the

Queensland captain and Essex dynamo. Buck and Law have masterminded many Queensland successes over the last four years, so the insights of arguably the best judge in the business were bound to be the most useful. Not many people have seen and studied Law with the same enthusiasm as Buck. Often the best opinion on a player's game comes from his coach, as he is the one who seeks to iron out any deficiencies or weaknesses.

That summation by one of the most astute and prepared coaches in the game was almost like the ultimate betrayal that the game can present. One minute, or at least one season, they are the closest of allies and then, due to the opportunities and circumstances of professional cricket, they are suddenly fighting against each other from opposite sides of the fence. 'You should bowl here because over the years that is where I have seen him dismissed most frequently, and if that doesn't work, I would suggest we attack him there because he is probably less comfortable in that area when he gets going.'

So that's how Western Australia will get him out next year in Australia. Very interesting. I must make sure to jot those words of wisdom down in my notebook. I'm sure my team-mates back home will find that very useful.

You can be sure I'll be taking my new-found knowledge back with me to Western Australia next summer. The only problem is that when Buck and I meet back on Australian soil, the roles will again be reversed. No longer will we be allies but instead, I can bet my last dollar that he will have plenty of ideas for his Queensland bowlers on how they should send me packing. All part of the mind game, I suppose.

I wonder what he will be saying and thinking about my game. An interesting thought! I will have to keep something up my sleeve so his bowlers don't get it too easy!

As so often happens, after ten overs our team meeting looked as though it may have been a futile affair. Law had smashed us to all parts of the smooth Chelmsford playing field.

So much for bowling where we said we were going to bowl. Bloody fast bowlers.

Luckily for the visitors, a ball shot along the ground, cartwheeling his off stump and immediately taking the heat off our opening bowlers.

Not exactly the way we had planned to get him out, but what the heck, that will do.

His legacy was followed by Nasser Hussain, who batted with the solidity of a brick and tile house in posting his first century of the summer. He is a very talented player who is quickly gaining a reputation as a great English fighter. Although he may not have been appointed England captain the other day, he still may captain his country in the future. I get the feeling he loves batting and won't give his wicket away for anything. A sign of a very good player.

Hussain's innings could have been enough for Essex, but in a game where they wasted two opportunities with the bat and ball, it was encouraging again to see the Middlesex guys persevering and eventually coming up trumps. Four in a row while not playing our best cricket is a positive sign for the summer.

It is a shame we had to get straight back on the motorway and make our way back to London. Once again a victory wasn't celebrated with anything more than a few handshakes, an encouraging word from the coach and a smile on the way back in the car. I hope this lack of team gelling won't affect our performances later in the season. Team spirit is such a vital part of any consistently successful team.

Saturday, 9 May – mad Welshmen!

Forget Australian Rules football junkies such as the Collingwood Magpies or Adelaide Crows supporters. Manchester United fans may compare, but I can't be sure. The Spice Girls have adoring fans who must come close, but even they are not quite so loud and boisterous. The Chicago Bulls spectators quite possibly compete in the adoration stakes, but I can't see them coming even close in the unadulterated art of sports spectating that I have witnessed today. Even the cricket-loving masses in India and Pakistan can't possibly compete for the mantle of number one sports enthusiasts with these wild men and women.

What, or more accurately who, you may ask, am I talking about? The Glamorgan County Cricket Club's extremely vocal spectators and fan club. After suffering their good-humoured support all day at Cardiff, it was very pleasing to hear their silence as Middlesex walked off the ground with another B&H win under our belts.

These Welsh cricket lovers definitely give any other supporters groups a run for their money when it comes to sheer enthusiasm and love for their heroes. Sure the numbers may not compete with Manchester United, the Chicago Bulls or the Spice Girls, but relatively speaking, the Glamorgan fans are extraordinary in terms of support for their team.

I'd hate to see them at a rugby game!

The championing and encouragement of 'their boys' presumably played a significant part in Glamorgan's Championship title last summer. Playing cricket in Cardiff against Glamorgan is like I imagine it to be playing football for Arsenal at Old Trafford. Even the strongest of warnings couldn't have geared me for this. Yes, I was warned before arriving this morning, and even though I vaguely remembered it from last summer, without any question the Welsh infatuation lived up to all expectations. In the heat of the battle, the constant ruthlessness of their barracking can be quite frustrating and daunting, but in hindsight, they provide a great atmosphere for a county cricket ground.

I wish they were on my side, though. I would rather they were my allies than my enemies any day!

After leaving Cardiff on the Australian team coach last year, I thought that maybe these Welsh cricket lovers simply had a dislike for the colonials. In a funny kind of way, it was good to hear the identical raucousness this afternoon. At least I now know that it doesn't matter who Glamorgan are playing; the opposition team, irrespective of the colour of the cap they are wearing, will be in for the equivalent reception.

Facing Waqar Younis in Karachi on a hot Pakistani afternoon is bad enough. There, you are facing the world's quickest bowler with rock-concert-volume screaming and banging occupying your auditory canals, while the dust from the dry pitch leaves you gasping for at least one breath of half-fresh oxygen. If facing his bowling isn't daunting enough, the atmosphere created by his adoring countrymen is definitely not for the faint of heart. The only difference between facing Waqar today at Glamorgan and during a match in Pakistan is that in Pakistan you can't understand what the spectators are yelling at you. One thing is for sure, the Glamorgan patriots, who seem to admire Waqar as much as his home supporters do, don't give you this small advantage; every single word of encouragement or abuse is as clear as the stars on a warm summer's evening.

The only saving grace for my team-mates and me was a great victory and a three-hour journey back to London with smiles on our faces. Keith Brown's second century of the B&H competition set up a stirring victory, and although the Welshmen replied with an incredible 120 off the first fourteen overs, we were able to peg them back and steal a rewarding two points.

Robert Croft, England's premier off-spinner, is making his mark on one-day cricket, not only with his bowling, but even more effectively by opening the batting for his team. His clean hitting has successfully set the scene and momentum for Glamorgan in the last few one-dayers. It is funny how many teams are following the Sri Lankan style of limited-overs cricket. A pinch-hitter and planned, aggressive stroke play in the first fifteen overs seem to be the trend now. This approach is undoubtedly becoming more prominent in English county cricket, and for that matter, throughout the international cricket world.

Styles of cricket, like anything, go through phases. When Australia were dominant in the late eighties and early nineties, they relied upon a solid start from Geoff Marsh and David Boon, with the emphasis placed upon aggressive running between the wickets and retaining wickets until the end. Sri Lanka's success in the last World Cup has reversed this trend with the accent now upon a whirlwind first fifteen overs.

It will be interesting to see the varying styles of one-day cricket at next year's World Cup and observe how the most successful teams go about their business. One thing we can all be sure about is that with every new strategy comes a responding combative strategy. I wonder which approach will be the most successful in the next twelve months? Again, the 1999 World Cup in England will act as the perfect stage to showcase the various methods adopted by the senior teams in international cricket.

The crowds, no matter who they are supporting, seem to love big shot-making, and that is one thing I can't see changing much in the near future.

Monday, 11 May – Cronje for Prime Minister!

The magnificent East Sussex golf course hosted a benefit golf day for the Sussex Young Cricketers today. I was on the invitation list, thanks to ex-Australian fast bowler Dave Gilbert who now works for the Sussex County Cricket Club. One of the luxuries of playing professional cricket in England is the opportunity to spend your few rest days honing your skills on some of the world's most beautiful golf courses. East Sussex certainly rates as one of the best-kept courses I have had the pleasure of playing. Even when your golf is as bad as mine, the chance to walk the fairways of such a fine course makes for a fantastic day.

It was Keith Brown's benefit dinner this evening at the Café Royal on Regent Street in the heart of London's West End. So after a fun day on the course, yet another adventure on the London roads offered us a further free mandatory tutorial in 'The Mastering of Navigation and Driving in England'. This time, Buck and I followed the London traveller's best friend, the *London A to Z* directory, and quite remarkably found our way to the plush restaurant's front door.

As I had been held up on the golf course, it was decided that instead of venturing home to shower and change into my dinner suit. I would ask Ian Gould, the Middlesex coach with responsibility for the county's cricket at all levels, to pick up my suit and bring it with him to the function. This was all set, but unfortunately when I arrived at the Café Royal attired in golf shorts and shirt, Ian was nowhere to be found. Here was I standing in the foyer looking more like one of the cleaners than one of the invited guests.

After a number of embarrassing meetings with the other formally dressed guests, 'Gouldy' eventually turned up carrying my suit bag and wearing a sheepish smile. When I finally found my way into the gentlemen's room. I hurriedly donned my immaculately dry-cleaned dinner suit only to find to my horror that there were no black dress shoes in the bag.

Oh my goodness gracious me, the embarrassment of it all, what am I going to do?

I had three options. One was to make a quick exit and come up with some lame excuse for missing the function. The second was to wear my brown leather shoes that I had worn home from the golf course, or thirdly, I could take a massive risk and wear the brightly coloured running shoes that I had worn while playing golf only hours before. Not much of a choice, but in the end I decided to take the riskiest option and go for the trend-setting approach to formal dining wear. With dinner suit and running shoes, I gathered myself and walked into the function with my chest pushed out, acting as though I was in total control of the situation. The truth is I felt like, and obviously looked like, a first-class plonker, but there was no way I was going to show it.

I could feel the stares coming from every angle, and comments were flying from all over, but in the end, nervously sweaty back and all, I got through the night. I had a big advantage, of course – I could get away with almost anything here in London because whatever I do it is generally excused with the saving comment, 'Don't worry, he is an Australian you know.'

Keith Brown's benefit dinner had an international flavour about it with members of the South African and England cricket teams providing the night's entertainment. South African captain Hansie Cronje, guest speaker for the occasion, was magnificent behind the podium. A career in politics should be considered after his playing days are over. He captivated the audience with the same touch as Jonty Rhodes captivates the public with his spectacular backward point fielding. He was able to recite poetry, use famous quotes from people from all walks of life and provide a humorous insight into life as the South African cricket captain. His fantastic speech was inspiring as he masterfully, yet humbly, set the scene for a successful benefit dinner. Tony Blair and Bill Clinton would have been proud of such a presentation.

I get the feeling that, by summer's end, my days will have been filled with a feast of cricket playing, while my few spare days will be taken up by a feast of benefit favours for Browny. Luckily, I have a very understanding wife, a cricket widow of the highest order.

CHAPTER FOUR

Warm-ups and Conveyor Belts

[illegible]

[illegible]

Wednesday, [illegible] May [illegible]

[illegible]

[illegible] Gordon, [illegible]

[illegible]

Wednesday, 13 May – team spirit?

Ball dominated bat on day one of the County Championship today. Three teams were bowled out for less than a paltry 150 and three of the other counties batting first scratched and clawed their way just past the half-respectable 200 mark.

Today's mediocre batting results were surprising, considering the luxury of the blazing sunshine around the country. For once this summer, a short-sleeved cricket shirt was all that was needed on a day that ironically seemed perfect for batting. Fast bowlers Devon Malcolm (Northants), Chris Lewis (Leicestershire), Dougy Brown (Warwickshire) and Andy Caddick (Somerset) all enjoyed at least five-wicket hauls, destroying this assumption.

The only team to dominate with the bat was the star-studded Surrey line-up. Mark Butcher and Alistair Brown helped themselves to centuries, while Alec Stewart, Graham Thorpe and the Hollioake brothers chipped in with good starts. Depending upon international selection, Surrey look likely to be the most dominant force in the competition, and in my eyes, will be the hardest team to beat during the summer. Their outfit is not unlike the NSW Blues back home. The deciding factor for Surrey will be their ability to adapt and form a team while their big guns are away on international duties. Whether they can cope remains to be seen. What I do know is that 'a champion team always beats a team of champions', and while Surrey look good on paper I won't be surprised to see them faltering at the business end of the season if they can't get this right.

Adam Hollioake is highly regarded as a strong captain, so I am sure he will know the benefit of his team bonding. I must admit, though, one thing I am noticing early in this county season is a lack of team spirit around the circuit. Some teams have it and it stands out very clearly. On first impressions, I won't be at all surprised to see teams like Leicestershire, Yorkshire and Lancashire using this to their distinct advantage this season.

Initial impressions suggest to me that English cricket doesn't really place enough emphasis upon a close team spirit and team bonding. In every successful team I have been involved in, this factor has been the glue that has held the team together and got us through both the good times and the hard times. The Australian cricket team motto involves 'helping out your mates, playing for the team, and enjoying your mates' success'. Under Australian captain Mark Taylor, this message has always been pushed very strongly and the essence of playing cricket as a team has always been the strength of arguably the world's number one Test-playing nation in the last four years.

In Western Australia, the motto painted all over

our changing-rooms reads: 'TEAM – Together Each Achieves More'. We try to stick with this plan to the letter and unsurprisingly we have been a very successful team over the last few years. John Buchanan is very strong on this concept of team building, but even at this early stage I feel he is fighting against some English barriers for his objectives. If he can build the Middlesex team spirit, and his ideas are grasped, I am sure we will enjoy great success.

Cricket is more than just a game played between bat and ball, and it is also more than just a means to earn an income. If more players in this country can see and understand that I feel they will not only be more successful but they will also enjoy playing the game a lot more. Enjoyment comes from success and generally success won't come unless everyone is pulling in the same direction; a vicious circle really, but one that will never disappear.

It is funny what you can start thinking about from a simple subject like Surrey's excellent batting today.

Friday, 15 May – Atherton is back

The big news today was the reportedly brilliant return to form of recently de-throned England captain Mike Atherton. Under enormous pressure from the English press, he must have slept better tonight knowing his position as England's senior opening batsman is secure. After a poor run of form in the West Indies and a well-publicised reign as England captain, the vultures were starting to circle what seemed to be a stumbling deer.

Atherton is held in the highest regard world-wide for his immense batting talent, and I am sure that newly appointed captain Alec Stewart will be thrilled knowing that he will go into the first Test against South Africa with his most experienced and reliable player full of confidence and back in supreme form. I was pleased for Atherton who is one of the finest batting technicians I have ever seen and a man who has played the majority of his Test career under the sort of pressure that few of us have experienced.

The fact he has made so many Test runs while captaining an often sinking ship is a credit to the Lancastrian's temperament and character. An England Test side without him opening the innings wouldn't seem right and would be a waste of one of the great players England have produced. I wouldn't be surprised to see 'Athers' have a fruitful summer now that the monumental pressure he has been subjected to over the last five or six years has been loosened like a slackened noose around his neck. The strength of a man's character often becomes clear when he is under pressure, and if today is any guide, Mike Atherton is as tough as old leather boots and a most worthy opening batsman in the Test match arena.

While Mike Atherton is sleeping easy tonight, my Middlesex team-mates and coach will also wake up tomorrow feeling fairly pleased with themselves. Today we had one of those dream days usually reserved for those sleeping hours under the covers. Starting the day 100 runs ahead of Somerset with seven wickets in hand, the game was evenly poised.

Fortunately for me, my first century at Lord's finally came – a dream come true for this colonial boy. Unless you fully understand and respect the game, the magnitude of batting well at Lord's is probably hard to comprehend. It is like a chocoholic having a free day out at the Cadbury's factory or an opera singer singing with Pavarotti; it is simply the ultimate in cricket experience in my view.

Batting with talented nineteen-year-old David Nash, who also made his first ton at the Mecca, we were able to guide Middlesex to a massive lead of 400. With twenty overs to bowl before stumps, any wickets were going to be a bonus, but thanks to aggressive spells from Angus Fraser and first-innings hero Richard Johnson, the Somerset top order crumbled, and at stumps they were 50 for 6. Everything we set out to achieve today had been accomplished. A success in itself!

From a personal point of view, it was something of a relief to walk back through the Long Room to extended applause. After experiencing the deathly Long Room silence that accompanies a couple of low scores, I can assure you the latter reception is far more pleasing.

Today has been one of those great days on the cricket field. Moments like these are to be cherished and enjoyed because you don't experience them every day. Today I understand more clearly why we play this great game. All the down days are quickly forgotten thanks to days like this.

At tea I was presented with my Middlesex cap, an earned honour, they tell me, for a county cricketer. There were a few raised eyebrows because I was presented with my cap after only three games, but what the heck; 233 not out in my first county game at Lord's should be some indication that I can play a bit.

* * *

I think I will try to stay out of the politics of the game, a demon, in my view, that seems to be so rife in sport.

It is going to take a bit of time to understand the English system of doing things. There seems to be a real seniority structure, which evidently originated in the olden days of professionals and amateurs. Obviously it is not as distinct in the modern game, but there are still examples within the dressing-room. Capped and non-capped players, for instance, wear different caps and sweaters according to their ranking, and change in different changing-rooms a lot of the time. This seems odd to me as I have been brought up in a system where you bust your gut to make the first team to earn the right to wear the team cap when you have been selected. It is almost a ceremony when a young player first plays for his state or country and dons the green gold Western Australian cap or baggy cap for the first time.

In contrast, when a player is selected to play for his county, until he has proven his worth he must wear a different cap and sweater and accept a lower pay structure. I can see the value in a player earning his stripes, but I believe when the team walks out on to the field they should all be in the same strip, proud to be a part of the team that they are representing. Generally, the newly selected player has been working to become a part of the team and therefore he should be made to feel a part of it.

Around the circuit, Warwickshire have already beaten Derbyshire; David Boon's Durham are in a strong position against Stuart Law and Essex; Kent and

Lancashire are in a stranglehold, even though Carl Hooper is on his way to a huge score; and the other games are evenly poised.

Saturday, 16 May – bloody warm-ups!

In a nasty twist of fate, enthusiasm and initiative worked against us this morning at Lord's. As we prepared to take the final four Somerset wickets and enjoy a relatively easy day, our mandatory morning warm-up turned into more of a bloodbath than an easy loosener of the weary muscles. So often the catalyst of a successful team, this time energy and enthusiasm had the opposite effect.

Trying to re-enact their more youthful years, our most senior team members had the ambulance sirens blaring through the St John's Wood streets as if they were screaming at each other above the remainder of the morning traffic. Among the sirens, screams and grimaces of our injured party was our physiotherapist, Simon Shephard, running around in a state of distress, knowing that his planned lazy weekend with his family was about to be ruined.

As a change from the mundane warm-up of jogging and stretching, a light game of touch rugby was planned. Unfortunately, our thirty-five-year-old wicketkeeper Keith Brown over-estimated the elasticity of his ageing hamstrings, and in his attempt to run a Will Carling-style try, pinged his left one. He could be out of action for a few games.

His misfortune was more destructive but far less humorous than a broken rib sustained by our firecracker coach John Buchanan. In his attempt to transform himself into Jonty Rhodes for the morning, he forgot the basic rule that his schoolboy days are now behind him. Joining in the fielding activities, he had the whole team laughing and enjoying his enthusiastic attempts at diving catches and acrobatic rolls; that is until his final effort at a fully stretched, right-hand 'screamer' left him sprawled out on the ground like a tripped soccer player. The crack of his rib was as loud as a cracking bullwhip, leaving poor old Buck in a horrible mess for the rest of the day and, if I know rib injuries, probably for the remainder of the season.

The sad result of this morning's misdemeanours, besides the obvious sustained injuries, is that tomorrow morning, we will more than likely have to go back to the same old boring warm-up routine. This is a shame because, as far as I am concerned, one of the worst parts of playing professional sport is jogging that first miserable lap of the cricket field every morning. Surely there are better ways to kick off the day's proceedings? The same old thing every morning! Admittedly retuning the body is an integral and important part of the day, but take it from me, it is also a very boring and painful part of a professional cricketer's day. It is hard trying to explain in words the physical and mental distress caused by a morning warm-up. It is that first lap that seems to take all the shine away from being a professional cricketer. Like trying to kick-start a motorcar that has a flat battery, you have to push yourself for the first few metres to give your body any chance of snapping into action.

After about thirty steps your feet, calf muscles,

quadriceps and hamstrings start to feel as though there is some elasticity creeping back into them from the day before. By the time you are halfway around the ground, your heart-rate has slightly increased, enough to open up your lungs, while three-quarters of the lap sees the first bead of sweat for the day popping its way out of the pores in your forehead. When you finally complete the circuit, it's the same routine again: 'OK boys, give your calves a good long stretch on the fence.' Then it's 'Now your hammys and quads, lads. Make sure you hold them for at least thirty seconds and do a couple on each leg.' I can hear the record player as clear as a summer sky. 'A couple of back rolls, fellas, and then give your back a good, long stretch on both sides.'

'Don't forget your shoulders and sides, especially you bowlers,' comes the cry from the physio. Honestly, it is the same routine every day and it doesn't matter whether you are playing for Middlesex, Western Australia, Australia or Scarborough CC in Perth, the routine never varies much from this. Every now and then, when the physio or coach decides to make things more fun, whammo, something goes wrong and it's back to the old routine.

I suppose it's not unlike the office worker who arrives at work and goes straight to the kettle for the first cup of coffee of the day. Sure, the cup of coffee and the first lap are designed to give you a kick-start but there is one major difference. With the first cup of coffee, you generally gain great satisfaction from sitting down and drinking it, the only downside being you rarely feel that good after the event. The aftertaste is bitter and your stomach starts to churn in protest. In contrast, I really don't enjoy one minute of a warm-up, but I do admit my body is always very appreciative of the fact that I am oiling it up for the activity ahead.

One thing I will never miss when I eventually retire from this game is the daily warm-up, as you can probably gather.

We could have taken the day's disastrous start as a negative sign from the cricket gods, but fortunately the day unfolded as expected, with the boys cleaning up the Somerset tail and taking the full points from the game. It took until after lunch to finish off the last four Somerset wickets, but a victory is a victory and a sweet reward for four good days of cricket at Lord's.

Opportunely, the early finish allowed the guys to enjoy the fever of the FA Cup final. Arsenal took the Cup 2–0 much to the disappointment of the Newcastle fans. Watching it live at 3.00 p.m. is far more enjoyable than sitting up at home in Australia, bleary eyed, sculling mugs of coffee, fighting off the sleep and yawns, in a generally futile attempt to witness one of the sporting calendar's biggest events. Until you have been in England on FA Cup final day, you can't truly appreciate the enormity of the day.

Adoring Arsenal and Newcastle fans, dressed in their club colours, hair dyed and throats hoarse, seemed to be enjoying the day, which incredibly quietened down the ever-buzzing streets of London. I thought AFL Grand Final day was big in Australia, but FA Cup final day is massive. The supporters thronging the streets and pubs celebrated the day as only the traditional English football supporter knows how. Driving through Hampstead, I was overawed by the singing and revelry associated with cheering on your football team. By the looks of it, there could be many sore heads come sunrise tomorrow.

Sunday, 17 May – the county cricket conveyor belt

Picture a tall, athletic man sitting in a sauna; he has been sitting there for twenty minutes and his arms are hanging by his side, face dripping, eyes red and posture slumped. You know the image – half-relaxed, sweating and drained of all energy. At 6.30 this evening, this was Middlesex's opening bowler Richard Johnson. We have just completed a Sunday League game and to say the least he is exhausted. After five days of competitive cricket, during which he has spent at least sixty hours at the cricket ground, he looks like a beaten boxer sitting in his changing-room corner. Although it looks like he's slumped in a sauna, 'Johnno', a genuine pace bowler, is actually sitting on his bench, shirt off, boots thrown, can of diet coke in his paw, withdrawn expression on his face. I am sure he is feeling every bit as tired as he looks, as I gaze over at him from my corner.

In the last five days he has worked his heart out, bowling aggressively for over fifty overs. He has also batted and fielded with the determination of a hungry lioness. Sure he's gained his just rewards by taking wickets and scoring his runs, but the fact is he knows in the back of his mind that after a day off tomorrow he will be expected to contribute with the same intensity on Tuesday. By summer's end, I think it will be this image that will remain with me for a long time as I remember life as a county cricket pro.

The feeling of success is sweet but it is so short-lived in this county game. Is there any time to reflect on a job well done? How can a Richard Johnson possibly recharge his batteries? Where is the time to reflect on the game that has just been played when tomorrow it starts all over again?

Add to the sheer quantity of his workload over the last week the scenario of today's game. It was an electrifying game decided on the last ball, a thriller in every sense of the word; a game played in front of a large Sunday afternoon Lord's crowd under a beating sun; a game of intense pressure that tested the character and nerve of every gasping cell in his young, fit body.

Although the excitement of the victory was tantalising and the celebratory atmosphere in the rooms was pumping, it will more than likely be the image of Johnno's screaming feet and tired eyes that will remain. How these English bowlers survive a full season has me guessing. Such an unnatural act on the body and yet these youngsters have to do it over after over to earn a living. The English system has the potential to produce some of the mentally toughest cricketers in the world. You have to have a mentality of cast iron to perform successfully and consistently day in and day out at this first-class level, and survive.

Unfortunately, the system also has the potential to burn out its players, both mentally and physically. How can a Richard Johnson be expected to storm in for his team five days a week for six months? Furthermore, Richard Johnson may one day be selected to play for his country. This honour will demand that he is in tip-top condition to bowl at his best for England. With his current workload, I can only wonder how fresh his legs and mind will be on his big day. No doubt his mind will be willing, but somewhere deep inside his grey matter will be a little voice crying out for mercy on his wearing body.

It really is a big ask!

Tuesday, 19 May – Crimewatch

Driving from Uxbridge Cricket Club, noticing the magnificence of the burning orange sun setting in my rear vision mirror, I couldn't help but think that the Middlesex cricket team should feature in the latest edition of *Crimewatch*. Why, you may ask.

If you happened to be watching or following the forty-over clash between Essex and Middlesex today, you would understand. So many times it has been said that cricket is a funny game, and if today is anything to go by, the old cliché is true. Like professional bank robbers, we literally stole a victory from Essex.

I have always maintained that it is difficult to chase a target, but at the thirty-second-over mark, with the visitors needing only 30 runs with seven wickets in hand, the fat lady's vocal cords were nicely warmed up. Fortunately for us, the fat lady seemed to strain her voice box in her final chorus and rather than singing Essex's merry tune, she faltered on the stage, tripping on her silver stilettos and leaving Middlesex victors by two runs.

With eight straight victories, Middlesex are looking strong in all forms of the game.

Derbyshire welcomed the return of Michael Slater today. He smashed 68, a relief for himself and his adopted club, who have been in the doldrums since their Aussie pro broke his hand in round one. I am sure 'Slats' will be looking forward to making up lost ground after a month out of the game. It must be disappointing for any county club when their overseas signing misses games through injury. Hopefully, Middlesex will get their money's worth with this Aussie pro.

CHAPTER FIVE
Hick's Achievement

Thursday [illegible] May [illegible] when [illegible]
[illegible]

[illegible]

[illegible] in [illegible]
[illegible]
[illegible] and [illegible] the [illegible]
[illegible] was [illegible] old [illegible]
[illegible] the [illegible]
[illegible]
[illegible] The [illegible]
[illegible] the [illegible]
[illegible]
[illegible]
[illegible]
[illegible]

[illegible]
[illegible]
[illegible]
[illegible] Playing [illegible] and [illegible] out for
[illegible] years without a break is a compliment to the
[illegible] of the man who is [illegible] like a good [illegible]

Thursday, 21 May – county to Test: what a leap!

Like two schoolyard bullies, Tom Moody and Graeme Hick took to our bowlers today. These two giants of the county circuit, both in physical stature and ability, slogged the leather cricket ball all round the ground. Such was the beating the poor old ball endured, I almost felt sorry for it. For the first time in my career, I didn't enjoy the sight of Tom's awesome power and ability. The way he pummels the cricket ball, particularly through the off side of the wicket, has given me immense pleasure over the years. His ability to control his innings like Bill Gates controls a laptop computer is generally a source of great delight to me as his runs keep the Western Australian scoreboard ticking over like a clock.

Now that I am experiencing county cricket first hand, I can fully comprehend the monumental workload Moods has exposed his body and mind to over the last decade. Playing cricket, season in and season out, for ten years without a break is a compliment to the resilience of the man who is ageing like a good red wine. If his supreme form in both countries is anything to go by, he seems to be improving with the years. I get the feeling, though, that if you took an X-ray of the big fella's body, you might find his backbone and leg bones out of true. His body must be pleading for a reprieve, even if it is only for a few weeks.

Guys like Tom, Courtney Walsh, Wasim Akram, Allan Donald, Carl Hooper and Waqar Younis are amazingly irrepressible characters, whose contribution to the game of cricket is immense. Playing all year round, as these guys have chosen to do, is a tribute to their dedication and love for the game.

Tom's partner in crime, Graeme Hick, was equally as lethal today. The man is a genuine run machine, who made his ninety-eighth first-class hundred look as easy as brushing his teeth in the morning. Ninety-eight first-class centuries is an indication of the man's class. Sure it was a flat wicket and we were lacking experience without Angus Fraser, but a century is a century and you can be assured this one was made with the precision of a brain surgeon. In anybody's language, Graeme Hick's dominance of county cricket is sure to remain in the annals of cricket history long after he leaves the game. He is often used as an example of a player who dominates county cricket but struggles to make the grade in Test cricket. In my view, anyone who can play with the intensity and power that I have just witnessed can make it at any level.

Having said this, I must admit one glaring aspect of today's play at Uxbridge was the potentially huge gap between county cricket and Test cricket. After one hour and twenty minutes, Hick, a world-class player in my opinion, and Worcestershire's young Test aspirant Vikram Solanki, were facing a couple of overs from part-time dobbler Richard Kettleborough. On a very flat pitch offering little to our opening bowlers, Mark Ramprakash had little option but to throw the ball to 'Ketts', who has bowled some medium pace in the past.

Test cricket provides intense pressure from the very first ball until the last ball before stumps. I am not sure today's first session was the perfect platform for either batsman to experience what they will be subjected to at the next level. Day one of a first-class game and after eighty minutes a part-timer is rolling his arm over. Give me a break! Can you imagine Graeme Hick walking in to bat on day one of a Test match against South Africa and after the first drinks break, Jonty Rhodes is thrown the ball by Hansie Cronje and asked to bowl a few overs to take the shine off the ball for the spinners. It would never happen would it?

Unfortunately, it happened today in county cricket and, like it or not, this is how English players are preparing for Test cricket. It is a pretty big jump. County cricket does not provide the tough finishing school required to prepare its pupils for the battlefield of Test match cricket.

Talking of the next level, the international one-dayer at The Oval was won by the visiting South Africans this afternoon. My gut feeling early in the series is that the South Africans may have too much discipline, desire and determination for England this summer. England will match their tough opponents man for man in talent but, in my eyes, it will come down to those little extras, the three 'd's, when it comes to the crunch. Matching the visitors in these one percenters will be the best way to ensure a hard-fought summer.

We will wait and see.

Friday, 22 May – dropped catches

Question: what is this? It is a little larger and heavier than an Australian dollar coin; it is a faded gold colour with the words *Decus et Tutamen*, meaning safety and honour, engraved around the edge; it is currently trading at a phenomenal rate to the Aussie dollar; and it has the face of Her Majesty the Queen on one side and the Royal coat of arms on the other. Answer: an English pound coin, of course. And I would have to say, I wouldn't mind having one for every time I have seen a top-class batsman dropped on a low score, only to go on to complete a big century for his team. It is almost an unwritten law of the game that states: 'When a top-class batsman is dropped early in his innings, he will go on to complete a century.'

I have seen it so many times that I would be a very wealthy man if a pound coin was donated to my retirement fund every time I have seen it happen in this crazy game. It happened in my first-class debut against Victoria in 1990–91 and it will probably happen in the last game of my career if my team-mates aren't all on their toes.

In that first Sheffield Shield game, I watched in horror as Dean Jones was dropped on 12. Another magnificent 222 runs later 'Deano' decided that he had imposed enough torture and edged one to Tim Zoehrer behind the stumps. Since those two horrendously long days in the Perth heat, the trend has continued to a most consistent tune.

Graeme Hick was dropped on the first ball he faced yesterday and it wasn't until 166 runs later that he decided to give us another chance. Talking in the clubhouse tonight, the subject of batsmen cashing in on a mistake was brought up and the consensus plainly shows how much the game of batting is played between the ears. My dad has been telling me since I was a little boy, 'The game is all in your head, son, it's all in your head.' I never really understood what he meant until I started playing first-class cricket.

Some people say batting has a lot to do with luck, but I find it very hard to accept that it is simply bad or good luck that determines your success. Those dreaded dropped catches seem to switch the player into action to do what they do best, bat and bat and bat. Some days even the greatest of batsmen aren't totally switched on to their task at hand. A let-off or reprieve from the opposition must work as a kind of alarm bell to wake the player up for the day ahead. Rarely do you see a top-line player given a chance without making the opposition pay for the mistake. The old adage about catches winning matches, oh how true it is!

There is no doubt that some days you start batting and your feet aren't moving quite as quickly as usual or you're not seeing the ball out of the bowler's hand as you'd like to. An early unpunished mistake can be the best thing for you, especially in county cricket, when it could be your third innings for the week, and your motivation and hunger aren't as high as they need to be when playing against first-class bowlers. Most good players have pretty big egos and the thought of not making the opposition pay when they have let you off the hook is enough to get those dancing feet and focused eyes attuned to what your brain and body know so well.

Although Hick's catch, a low one at cover, was a tough one, we paid dearly for it today. Moods finally declared Worcestershire's first innings at 627, which included three individual centuries, and 140 overs of fielding on a very flat pitch. They say 'cricket is a great game but batting is a better one' and after two days on the Uxbridge playing field I can see what they mean. My feet feel like blocks of molten lava and I can't help but wonder how Mike Gatting's old feet are going.

It is not only Gatt's feet that are screaming tonight in the changing-room. Also suffering after two of the longest days of cricket I have ever endured are the deflated egos of our bowlers who have just bowled themselves into the ground for very little reward. If Richard Johnson was physically and mentally drained a few days ago, how do you think he is travelling now?

I don't know how he can possibly make it through the season at this rate. This workload is incomprehensible.

By the look of the scores on Teletext, our game wasn't the only one to produce a shed full of runs. There were huge scores all around the country, but none like that achieved by Northants opening batsman Malachy Loye who will arrive at the ground tomorrow morning to see 232 not out on the scoreboard. How good do you think he will be feeling when he walks out for his warm-up, seeing his name on the scoreboard with 232 perched next to it – that's the stuff of dreams.

Middlesex now have two days to bat for our lives in an attempt to salvage this game of cricket. Maybe a dropped catch will help my weary legs get through the next two days of batting, or maybe the motivation of seeing another pro on the verge of 300 will be enough to pump me up.

Saturday, 23 May – a nightmare dismissal

Well, that's the last time I play Mr Nice Guy with the opposition.

Doing the right thing by my Western Australian captain, I asked him over for dinner last night. Over a take-away curry and glass of Australian red, he warned me of his gut feeling that he would get me out with his wily off-spinners today. Knowing that he bowls pretty ordinary 'offies', I laughed at his poor excuse for a joke, and bet him a crate of red wine that I would make a century before he even got close to sending me back to the Uxbridge pavilion. By the time I had reached the nervous nineties, Moods finally brought himself into the attack, not off his pretend spin bowler's run-up, but rather off his more accustomed long run. After pulling him to the boundary for four, the scoreboard told me that I was only two runs short of my century.

Seeing the ball like the proverbial football, and batting on a very flat pitch, I could already picture myself proudly receiving the twelve bottles of red wine that we had agreed upon. With a sheepish grin on his face, Moods ran in to bowl, and delivered a 'pie' down the leg side. Unfortunately, in my obvious preoccupation with an expected victory, I let my concentration lapse for a single moment, nicking the ball to the wicketkeeper.

I can't believe it. Anybody but Tommy!

As I trudged off the ground, with the memory of my Aussie team-mate's joyous face etched in my brain, I figured that the only way I would escape from paying my bet was on a technicality. After all, he had bragged that he would send me packing with his spinners. I know that he is a very handy medium pacer, so my excuse will centre around the fact that I was actually abusing his lack of ability as a spin bowler rather than as a bowler full stop.

But whether I lose the bet or not, Tom will be happy anyway, knowing that for ever after he will be able to say, 'Remember that time at Uxbridge when I got you out for 98?' Easiest wicket he's ever taken he told me after the game. What a bloody nightmare!

Tuesday, 26 May – single Mr Mum!

In the ants' nest public transport system of London known as the tube, I made my Green Park link with only seconds to spare. Sweating and panting and holding my fourteen-month-old daughter under my arm, the train door snapped closed behind us. Relieved at making my required link, I fell into a spare seat and talked baby-talk with Jessica, congratulating her on winning her first 200-metre sprint. As I settled into playful banter with my little girl, I had to look twice at the gentleman directly opposite me. It was none other than Jonty Rhodes. Amazing! In a place the size of London, it seemed almost absurd that a fellow cricketer and mate happened to be on the same train, in the same carriage, at exactly the same time.

It was nice to catch up, albeit for a few minutes, with one of the game's great blokes. He was telling me the South Africans were happy with their one-day victories and that they were now looking forward to getting stuck into the Test series. Although he had played well in the one-dayers, he was feeling a little disillusioned, as it seemed unlikely that he would be selected for the first Test team. He was worried that, although the South Africans would be in England for another two months, his tour was as good as over.

Having been in his shoes many times for Australia, I could sympathise with his concern, but offered him the friendly advice of hanging in there and taking the opportunity if it came. With a smile, the one that permanently lives on his face, we shook hands and he jumped off at his stop.

After Jonty had gone, the crowds started to grow as the peak hour started to tick into overdrive. Having to change trains, I made my way up and down escalators, eventually pinpointing my final West Hampstead destination. In the centre of a hot and humid carriage, holding my baby, a pram and a backpack, I found myself leaning against people of all colours, shapes, attitudes and sizes. For a brief moment, I began to realise how hard it must be for a single mum. I'd left my wife and her best friend for a spot of shopping, and a visit to the theatre in Leicester Square, promising them optimistically that returning home with Jess would be a breeze. I was starting to regret it as soon as we'd bade farewell.

With the sweat starting to drip down my back and my agitated little girl crying out her hysterical protests at not being allowed to run around the packed train, I was starting to feel like I was in a scene from the movie *Scream*. With two stops to go, Jessica's whimpers had turned into screams and sobs, a racket that would break your heart! The crowd stared accusingly at me as though I was a terrible father, but what was I to do? Pathetically, I grinned my way past the staring eyes and did my best to amuse my hot and aggravated daughter.

When the train door finally crashed open at West Hampstead, the relief was even greater than seeing the end of a Curtly Ambrose spell. If twenty minutes in a crammed sauna known as a London tube wasn't enough, my problems escalated when I jumped off the train to be greeted by black clouds and pouring rain.

Do I sit and wait or do I make a one-kilometre dash for my lovely dry apartment? The demons in my mind were warning me about pneumonia for the both of us, slipping on the slippery roads and horrified mothers. The angels were advising me that I surely couldn't stand here until it stops raining. It never stops raining in this bloody place and besides I had run out of games to play with Jess.

It was time to put my fitness into action. After a monumental run, we arrived home, both soaking wet and worse off for our day in London, but surely closer for the experience. Just like changing a dirty nappy, this rest day taught me that facing a fast bowler on a green, seaming pitch is nowhere near as hard as being a single dad in the centre of London.

Goodbye Mr Mum!

Wednesday, 27 May – quarter-finals of the Benson & Hedges Cup

From my seat in the Lord's changing-room, I am confronted by two of all cricket lovers' greatest pet hates. One is the growling, black clouds up above and the second is the *Star Trek*-style HoverCover that is being manoeuvred surgically by groundsman Mick Hunt and his willing workers; both mean rain, and rain means no cricket.

Reflecting on this uncontrollable factor, I quickly come to one conclusion. Having been in England for a month or so, I am becoming immune to the frustrations of heavy precipitation, but I can't admit to the same tolerance for some of the rules being formulated in county cricket. To my horror, I have just learnt that the result of this game may be decided by something called a 'bowl-off' tomorrow evening. This potentially comical way of deciding who wins and who loses this prestigious one-day quarter-final by default seems absurd – five bowlers hitting or missing a set of stumps to decide a game of cricket. The concept at first makes the brain hit seven on the Richter scale.

Already this fifty-over contest can be extended to two full days of play, an allowance to compensate for any rain delays. Even ten overs per team will be accepted as a full game, but in the event of two days of heavy rain and a total washout, the penalty shoot-out will come into play.

Knowing this, our warm-up this morning, as the drizzle continued to dampen the waterlogged outfield, constituted a practice bowl-off between our eleven possible stump-hitting candidates. Surprisingly, the five selected players consisted of wicketkeeper Keith Brown, opening batsman Richard Kettleborough, Gus Fraser, skipper Mark Ramprakash and myself. This dibbly-dobbly crew of pie-throwers (Gus excepted) could help to get us through to the semi-final.

It seems bizarre to me that a game of cricket can be decided like this. I'm sure I am supposed to be playing professional cricket in England, not professional soccer.

Fortunately, by 4.45 p.m. the ground had half-dried and Ramps had won the toss leaving the Essex batsmen to face the music on a lively Lord's pitch. As the big hand ticked over to twelve and the small hand to eight, Essex had scrambled to a very respectable 232 off their fifty overs. Stuart Law and youngster Stephen Peters, who looks a very promising prospect, were the stars of the day, controlling the Essex innings on a difficult pitch.

Middlesex will have to bat very well tomorrow to advance to the semi-finals on 9 June. As long as the rain stays away, and a full fifty overs is attained, the best team will be the rightful semi-finalists. This is the best scenario; it would be a shame to see a novelty result producing a winner after a month of competitive and tense one-day action.

As with the Duckworth-Lewis scoring system, there must be a better way. Maybe the team finishing the preliminary rounds with the better record should go through to the semi-finals. A penalty shoot-out may work in soccer as a last resort; after extra time has been played, it creates tension for the huge crowds and tests the nerve of all participants. In cricket, though, a bowl-off seems an unfair method of deciding a winner for a lucrative competition such as the Benson & Hedges Cup. As the saying goes, 'it's just not cricket'. I am just glad I am not an administrator who has to find the best answer to these questions.

Thursday, 28 May – a loss

Letting Essex off the hook in the last ten overs yesterday cost Middlesex dearly today. Rather than chasing just under 200 on a sporting wicket, we instead found the Essex total of 232 beyond our grasp. We made tough work of a competitive but achievable total, as we fell 20 runs short. In a disappointing end to an excellent Benson & Hedges Cup series, it will be frustrating watching the semi-finals in a fortnight's time.

Trying to find something positive from the result, I am glad that it wasn't decided by a bowl-off. The best side on the day now progresses, while at Middlesex we lick our wounds and prepare for the NatWest series in June. After beginning the season with such promise, I hope this isn't the start of a slide.

Even though we had our best team playing, we lacked the intensity to beat a side that we have already beaten twice this summer. Essex won the big moments in this game, stealing the initiative when we were seemingly in control. They say in sport you can't give the opposition a sniff or you will pay the penalty. We have paid the penalty over the last two days.

The semi-finals of this trophy, the last time it will be contested in county cricket, will be played between Yorkshire and Essex, with the all-star Surrey line-up taking on Leicestershire on Tuesday, 9 June. If I was a betting man, I'd have my money on a Yorkshire versus Surrey final at Lord's.

Friday, 29 May – the spirit of Lord's

When the opportunity arose to play county cricket with Middlesex, the allure of having Lord's as my home ground was too great to refuse. The luxurious changing-rooms, the Long Room, the waterfall shower-heads, historic pavilion, lush bowling-green outfields and five-star à la carte lunch menu were all incredible bonuses to be enjoyed.

It is only now, when I feel a part of the Middlesex CCC, that I am beginning to realise that the real catch of Lord's is not the sweet, physical fruits but rather an invisible spirit or feeling, hard to describe respectfully in words. I could call it 'atmosphere', but this term is almost too generic to describe the spirit which makes cricket's Mecca so enticing. It is a spirit which grabs you from the moment you set foot in the Long Room, where the museum setting that houses beautiful old paintings of village cricket, bygone days and portraits of the game's greatest-ever players, embraces you like an old friend.

After the tossed coin fell the wrong way up this morning, the prospect of another long day in the field was potentially daunting. By stumps, however, this blow had been surprisingly softened by the mere experience of spending 104 overs under the watchful eye of the terracotta-coloured, grandpa pavilion. Fielding is never the greatest of pastimes, especially in county cricket, so any day that can be as easy and enjoyable as this one is greatly appreciated.

Two weeks ago, I spent an almost identical day of cricket on the less hallowed turf of the Uxbridge Cricket Club. The same number of overs were bowled, the pitch was comparably flat and the result of a few wickets for hundreds of runs was repeated. Like magic, though, today passed like Christmas day, as that Lord's spirit saw me through like an old mentor. Where my encounter with Uxbridge felt like twenty hours squeezed into a six-and-a-half-hour day, the clock simply seems to tick faster at cricket's version of heaven. All I can put it down to is the magical spirit of Lord's.

Saturday, 30 May – a tribute to Hick

One hundred hundreds! It just doesn't seem right. Even my mum gasped in disbelief when I told her of this amazing achievement. Considering she is no aficionado of the game, that is saying something in itself.

For an Australian Sheffield Shield player, one hundred first-class games is something of an achievement. To talk of one hundred first-class centuries is frankly beyond comprehension. To play one hundred first-class games in Australia, a player needs to have ten injury-free seasons, not to mention consistent good form and a dedicated desire.

With this in mind, I attempt a few mental calculations

sitting here on the Lord's balcony. The highest number of Sheffield Shield centuries scored by a Western Australian batsman is twenty-four by Geoff Marsh. A respected Test player and Western Australian run machine, he ended his career playing 112 Shield games, averaging over 40. Mulling over Graeme Hick's achievement today, I realise that Swampy Marsh's twenty-four centuries pretty well fade into insignificance. One hundred times Graeme Hick has walked to the crease with a duck sitting on his shoulders, and one hundred times he has eliminated that dreaded duck with his Duncan Fearnley or Slazenger blade, and marched past cricket's golden figure. Quite an awesome achievement when you think about it.

I remember being in England early in his career when he was tagged the next Bradman. His sheer weight of runs then seemed comparable to the world's greatest-ever batsman. Touted as England's 'great white hope', as he qualified to play Test cricket for his adopted country, his ratio of centuries to innings was quite breathtaking and inspirational. Now that I have played against him, I can see that it is also his presence at the crease that adds to the enigma of one of county cricket's greatest players. His crunching power off both feet has left many a bowler and cover fieldsman quaking in their boots; the prospect of another Hick annihilation is almost soul destroying.

The *Cricketers' Who's Who* tells me he has played over 350 first-class games, meaning his conversion rate is just over a century every three and a half games. Knowing the discipline, technique, concentration and desire required to score a first-class century, Hick's colossal performance is simply monumental.

Twenty-three other players have matched this splendid milestone. The distinguished list includes such greats as Sir Donald Bradman, Denis Compton, Sir Len Hutton, Jack Hobbs, Vivian Richards, Sir Colin Cowdrey, Geoff Boycott and Graham Gooch, to name just a few. To be added to such a band of players must be an honour for the thirty-two-year-old run machine born in Rhodesia.

Although the feat was inevitable at the start of this season, the way he passed the milestone is a further tribute to his dominance of county cricket. Today was his fourth consecutive championship hundred, an outstanding feat in itself.

Tom Graveney, another proud member of the hundred hundreds club, toasted Hick with a glass of bubbly at the beautifully picturesque Worcester Cricket Club. Like Sir Gary Sobers saluting Brian Lara after breaking the world record, it was significant to see two members of this privileged club standing in the middle of the superb Worcester ground, enjoying a brief moment in the history of our great game.

Talking to many wise heads around the circuit, the educated opinion seems to be that Graeme Hick will be the last member of the famous club. With fewer domestic games and more international commitments, it will take a Herculean effort for another player to surpass the milestone.

Will Graeme Hick be the last? There are two things I know about this question. One is that my Middlesex team-mate and English cricket icon Mike Gatting is still batting like a hungry tiger as he pursues the distinction. He has eight to go, a tough achievement, but one that is not beyond his grasp. The second is that this little left-handed colonial boy, while keen in mind and body, will never get close; not from lack of desire but rather from lack of opportunities and probably ability.

Salute Graeme Hick.

CHAPTER SIX

A Break . . . For More Rain

Wednesday, 3 June – unleashed, Stephen Harmison

To quote my good mate and run machine Matty Hayden, 'Sometimes you go out to bat and it feels like you have got someone else's hockey stick in your hands. You know, it just doesn't feel right.'

Today my friend's philosophy on poor form, or a bad day in the middle, rang true as I pushed and nudged, played and missed, and took as many blows to the body as one of Prince Naseem's unfortunate opponents. Falling into bed tonight I had more bruises on my ribs, thighs and buttocks than you would wish on your worst enemy. It was just one of those bad days at the office, a day that inevitably happens when you play so much cricket, but one that you never look forward to.

With every passing delivery I could hear Haydo's voice ringing through my embarrassed ears. To put it mildly, I felt like a complete novice standing in the middle of Lord's, looking as though I had been employed by Middlesex as an opening bowler or groundsman rather than a professional batsman.

The intriguing aspect of this infatuating game is the

changing faces that it presents every day. Crazy as it seemed today, it was only two days ago that I ran ecstatically from Lord's having just scored 153 not out and guided the team to a fantastic victory against Glamorgan. Just two days ago, I played an innings in which every ball seemed to hit the middle of the bat and my hands, feet and bat were working together with the precision and timing of a Tag Heuer wristwatch.

When you think you are starting to master the art of batting, the game has a knack of coming back and pulling you into line.

After winning the toss, I found myself back out in the middle at Lord's, batting on a pitch that seemed to have more life than the one we had finished on, on Monday. Nevertheless, the pitch shouldn't have made that much difference to the way I was seeing the ball, but it looked more like a garden pea than the hot-air balloon I was seeing on Monday afternoon. Maybe it was the anticipation caused by David Boon's comment to me as we walked on to the ground at the start of play. After wishing me a good morning and extending a short 'Good luck,' he grinned at me and grunted, 'Wait until you see what I have to unleash on you today young fella.' With this, my curious mind began to tick over.

I had heard all about a young, fiery spearhead named Melvyn Betts. In the first over, he rocketed the new ball into my rib cage, crashed a yorker into my big toe and had me caught behind ducking a bouncer off a no-ball. He was good, but still I could see 'Boony' smiling like a proud assassin from first slip. What in heaven's name could Boony have up his sleeve that was making him so excited. All week, head groundsman Mick Hunt had been promising that this pitch would be quick and bouncy. Maybe he was simply pleased to be playing on a pitch that was more reminiscent of an Australian one, but then again, surely that couldn't be it. I wonder what Boony is on about? Whatever it is, he had my mnd racing.

After surviving the initial barrage from Betts, I could see from the corner of my eye a tall, lanky lad with an innocent, baby face and long hair swinging his arms, jogging on the spot and jumping up and down like a monkey in the zoo. Obviously warming up to bowl the next over, I thought nothing of it until I glanced at Boony who was still grinning like a circus clown. As he walked past me at the end of the over, he winked at me as if to remind me of his early promise, or threat.

I wasn't to be disappointed. Unleashed was Stephen Harmison, a six-foot-three nineteen-year-old from Northumberland in the north-east of England. Luckily, I was standing at the non-striker's end when this unlikely looking lad ambled in, jumped high at the crease and, from over seven feet in the air, delivered a bouncer which thudded into the gloves of his keeper. To everyone's surprise, except Boony's, the ball hit the gloves before any of us could blink. Boony's grin glistened as my eyes widened at the prospect of battling this youngster, whose baby face had quickly turned into that of a fierce-eyed monster. His first ball wasn't a fluke, as the next six overs produced some of the fastest bowling I have faced for a long time. This boy was quick, and I mean really quick. Like a West Indian fast bowler, he bounces in, hits the crease hard and hits the pitch harder.

Although he was a little wayward, he is an exciting prospect for Durham and possibly England, and most certainly a name for the future. With England selectors Mike Gatting and Graham Gooch watching the game from the pitch and the balcony respectively, I would be surprised if his name hasn't been pencilled into their cerebral notepads.

He is not exactly the sort of bowler you particularly like to face to feed your family, but then again, his type of aggressive and exciting bowling is exactly what county cricket needs. He is different. He gets you off the front foot and reminds you with every ball that a moment's lack of concentration on your part is potentially a broken finger or rib or, even worse, a broken wicket.

Now I could understand Boony's enthusiasm. There is nothing like standing in the slips with a young fast bowler steaming in, threatening the opposition batsman. The West Indians must have the time of their lives every time they walk on to a cricket field with four express fast bowlers in their line-up.

The question is, how long can a young man like Stephen Harmison continue to maintain this exciting raw pace? As the days turn into months, and the overs build up, I only hope for cricket's sake that the jump remains as high, and the hunger to frighten batsmen remains the same. If he is managed well by David Boon, this grinning assassin has an awesome career ahead. He is a name for the future. The big question is will his body be able to survive the constant demands of county cricket? If he does, look out any batsmen who may be reading these lines. I can testify to his pace and potential – witness my bruised fingers typing these lines.

Thursday, 4 June – Boony

As David Boon strode out at Lord's this afternoon, I couldn't help but smile, in awe I guess, at this determined little bastard making his way to the middle of this privileged cricket ground. So long a boyhood hero and now a good mate, it seemed odd, seeing one of Australian cricket's great ambassadors, trudging to the crease wearing a Durham CCC helmet rather than his favourite baggy green Australian cap.

During his three hours of crease occupancy, his favourite pastime, many of my Middlesex team-mates asked me about Boony, as he cut and drove his way to yet another first-class half-century. What's he like? Is he as scary as he looks? Is he a legend in Australia? Did he really drink that many cans of Foster's on the way to England? The questions kept coming.

With every answer, I just smiled, knowing that this man, all five foot seven of him, personifies Australian cricket and is perhaps what English cricket needs. He's the sort of bloke you would take to the trenches with you. He's tough as old leather, loves the game and would never let you down. He loves his country and is rightfully proud of his achievements, on and off the field.

They say he did drink all those cans on the way to England, a feat that just adds to the legend of one of the game's greatest fighters. Let's face it, you would have to fight through a few pain barriers to break such a drinking record. Certainly a gutsy effort if you ask me. Marathon runners are a breed of their own, but anyone who can drink forty-odd cans of lager without a break between Melbourne and London is mentally tougher than any marathon runner that I have ever met.

Hopefully for Middlesex's sake we won't be seeing too much more of D.C. Boon tomorrow. Maybe a few glasses, or even bottles, of red wine tonight will slow him down for the morning. I am sure it won't take too much enticing, especially if I ask Sue to buy a couple of the best bottles of red she can find. As much as I have enjoyed watching him bat over the years, I think, for once in my life, I'd rather see him shuffle across his stumps and miss a straight one, before he does any more damage to our bowlers.

Another top-class opening batsman confirmed his status today. On day one of the first Test against the South Africans, Mike Atherton validated why he is likely to leave the game as one of England's greatest-ever opening batsmen. Walking from Edgbaston at four minutes past six o'clock, with 103 runs to his name, England's captain for the last half-decade had proved to his detractors why he must lead his team-mates at the top of the England batting order.

Technically Athers plays as straight as a shiny gunbarrel and his power of concentration rivals that of the most talented micro surgeon. He has once again passed the test and distinguished himself as a cricket warrior of the highest order.

England couldn't have hoped for a more positive start to this important Test series. With a new era in English cricket once again being promised, a single fallen wicket in three full sessions is a grand start. Debutant England captain Alec Stewart will be hopeful that more days under his leadership will prove as fruitful. All that went wrong was the loss of the toss. Not a bad downside for the newly appointed skipper and his talented team who are desperate to win their first five-Test series in twelve years!

Monday, 8 June – too much cricket?

Like ice-blocks thawing, my weary legs slowly began to lose their stiffness by about four o'clock this afternoon. As a treat, I assigned my body a rare reward of a complete day of rest and relaxation. Out of the last sixteen days, yesterday was my fourteenth day of cricket. Not only do my feet, legs and back ache, but also my mind was starting to wander and eat away at my ambition and hunger for the next day of play. This is very regrettable as I pride myself on playing the game with the hunger and determination of a scorned woman.

As I woke this morning it was almost a relief knowing that I didn't have to play cricket and put up with the related pressures. Acting like a zombie, and only having to deal with the pressure of babysitting for a couple of hours, I have a few days to reinvigorate my cricket soul and refuel the dwindling fire. This break couldn't have come at a more opportune time; I am starting to agree with the popular consensus that English cricketers play far too much cricket. The itinerary is very hectic and although I couldn't wish to be living a better lifestyle, a day off here and there almost feels like Christmas.

In 1987 while visiting England as a schoolboy cricketer, I was billeted by the Bicknell family from Surrey. I vividly remember the feeling of envy as I watched Darren and Martin playing the game day in, day out as professional county cricketers. I couldn't understand for the life of me why they both had to be dragged out of bed, protesting and complaining, on one particular July morning eleven years ago. Now the truth is starting to be revealed.

They, like so many of their colleagues, have been doing the circuit and living this lifestyle for well over a decade. I have been doing it for less than two months and I can now appreciate more clearly their moments of torment and complaint. When I return to Australia, the last sixteen days will really stay in my memory. In a culture where we play our cricket on the weekends, or a Sheffield Shield match every two or three weeks, this extended run of cricket is so very foreign. I can see it already; when people ask me about English cricket my first response will likely be they play too much. If you give a child one Mars bar he will eat it with glee. The next one will also taste good, but as you keep handing over more and more Mars bars, the child will eventually lose the taste and hunger for them. In my opinion the same can happen in county cricket. West Indian Jimmy Adams, who played a season for Nottinghamshire, told me that he loved the first three months of county cricket but hated the last three months. It is a terrible realisation that I found it hard to get out of bed yesterday morning and that I am enjoying my day off so much.

Cricket is hard enough to play as it is, let alone if you are playing it without hunger for success or the motivation to give a hundred per cent energy every time you enter the arena. Of course you always want to do well, but if your motivation is dwindling you are doing yourself and the game an injustice. For county cricket and its assets, the quantity of fixtures can lead to mediocrity, a dirty word in professional sport.

My only question now is that if the Bicknells found it hard to get out of bed as teenaged professionals, how do they get out of bed these days? The mind boggles!

Tuesday, 9 June – public dunnies

Bloody amazing! Of all the places to find a clean dunny I would have least expected to discover it at the dirty and old Finchley tube station. Let's face it, going to a toilet in a public place is a daunting prospect at the best of times.

After a couple of afternoon cappuccinos, and a great chicken vindaloo last night, I was unfortunately left with no choice but to scramble for the nearest convenience before boarding my tube this afternoon. The fact was that my stomach started echoing painful warning alarms and my legs began turning to jelly as I scampered up the steps of Finchley station. The thought of relief in a tube station toilet block was a very scary proposition, but what choice did I have when I was four stops and a ten-minute walk from home?

Germs on the seat, no toilet paper, vile, stale odour and the remains of the last occupant grotesquely staring at you when you lift the plastic lid – a scene that could only resemble your worst horror movie was what I was imagining, enough to make your skin crawl, as I burst through the door marked 'Gentlemen'. To my genuine surprise, the horror movie turned out to be more like a classic Andrex toilet paper commercial with the cool breezes, fluffy white puppy dogs and pristine tiled floors. My nightmare turned into a moment of bliss as I crashed open the toilet door, ripped off my belt and collapsed on to the flimsy but unimpeded seat. The water was blue and clear, the seat white and new, and the air was astoundingly fresh. Like a king on his throne, I could have been anywhere in the world, sitting back and enjoying my emergency afternoon appointment with nature.

As I left to catch the tube, I couldn't help but marvel at this new discovery in my life. From today forth, I have a new ally and friend. The next time I feel the need to use a toilet, or even if I feel like escaping the hustle and bustle of London for a few moments of private consultation, I have a safe and happy haven to call upon at any time. I will now pay my taxes less grudgingly, as I can see that my money is obviously being spent on a very good cause: the excellent maintenance of the public toilet system in London. This is a tremendous way to spend my hard-earned cash, even if it has to save me only once a year. Bravo!

They say you learn something every day and I have to admit today's lesson leaves me with a smile on my face, which I can't say for so many of the lost-looking souls so serious in beautiful and historic London town.

Saturday, 13 June – a plea to the sun

Have you ever noticed that the trees start looking like wet, shaggy sheepdogs after a long rainfall? Early in the afternoon, the old, red-leafed oak outside our bedroom window stood as proud as a university graduate, enjoying the summer rain and growing stronger with every drop. Now, in the early evening, it looks more bedraggled than proud, with the continuance of this persistent rain. It's almost as if the tree is hanging its head, or in this case its leaves, in protest at the last three hours of rain.

This discontent is being felt universally. The tree is not the only one fed up with the bleak skies, icy temperatures, wet footpaths and sodden Hampstead streets. Try explaining to your fourteen-month-old daughter that we can't go outside for a walk because it is too cold and too wet. It is like trying to explain to Mike Gatting that he can't have his obligatory bacon sandwich every morning. Good luck! And so much for spending my day off on Hampstead Heath with a picnic basket, eating ice-cream (or what they call cornets over here), and relaxing under the summer sun. Isn't it meant to be summer?

Everyone politely and optimistically promised me that summer will be a scorcher this year. 'It always is after the cold April we are having,' they predicted. Well, sorry, but I am sure summer was meant to have started about a month ago.

My mother-in-law, visiting the UK for the first time, asked me today, in an honest and inquiring tone, 'Justin, is the sky always grey in London?' What am I supposed to say? Of course, I know that English summers can be like heaven with glorious blue skies, mild temperatures and the magnificent twilight period, but come on, summer, you are letting me down.

Give us a break, weather gods. Fair's fair, the gardens must have had their share of rainfall. It is surely time to re-test the thermometers, pack away the woollens and let the sun-starved

English men and women, and their visitors, start working on their sun tans. You will make a lot of people happy. The streets are just too quiet under these bleak June skies.

So much rain can't be great for the spirit. The only bright side is that I personally am not missing any cricket on my day off, but by the look of the Sky Sports cricket scoreboards on the Internet, most of the games have been abandoned for the day. Once again I say, 'Rain, rain, go away!'

Sunday, 14 June – more rain

Grey skies all the way up the M1, grey skies all the way back. Not the perfect conditions for today's proposed Sunday League fixture in Derbyshire. One hundred and twenty miles up the motorway is a long way to travel to find a ground waterlogged and unfit for play. One hundred and twenty miles back to London is even harder to come to terms with, without a single ball having been bowled.

It took two hours of card games and tennis-ball cricket in the dressing-room to help pass the time before the umpires and captains agreed to abandon today's fixture. Having lost my money on the cards, and some of my pride with the tennis ball, it was time to head back to London. This travelling isn't something I will miss about county cricket.

Yesterday's impassioned plea to the weather gods obviously didn't work as the rain continues to show its ugly and bleak face. Knowing that Northampton have fast-men Devon Malcolm and Franklyn Rose, my prayers are increasing as I am not that keen to take on these speedsters on a green, damp track come Wednesday.

After a few enjoyable days off, Wednesday marks the end of my rest period for the summer and the continuation of the season's campaign. Sorry, legs!

Monday, 15 June – hooligans and dentists

What a day! All morning Heart FM announced how the tube strike, torrential rain and employee absenteeism resulting from England's first game in the football World Cup were sure to slow things up on the roads. They got it right! I spent half the day sitting in traffic jams, shouting and cursing and watching loyal England supporters of all ages and sizes walking the streets wrapped in England flags, singing 'England, England, England . . .'

Imagine if Glenn Hoddle's men win a few games and progress through to the final rounds. If today is any indication, this country will come to a total standstill. Every pub in England was heaving from midday and the radio was talking about understanding bosses and beer and pizzas in the offices. All this hoohah for round one against Tunisia, not the greatest of soccer nations.

Unfortunately, the news making international headlines was not the actual game between England and Tunisia but rather the shameful pictures of England's hooligans in France; a sorry sight if I say so myself. These idiots, visitors to another country, fought, skulled beer and showed blatant disregard for everyone but themselves on the streets and outside the bars in France.

These guys are hardly worth the sincere apologies being made by England's diplomats to the French people and authorities.

Their behaviour is a sad portrayal of a minority of England football lovers. The ones who missed the boat to France made up for it in England, terrorising some pubs in North London. Driving along Whetstone High Road in North Finchley, I nearly ran over one shirtless drunken idiot wearing a red wig and tattoos. After missing him, his shaven-headed mate, who would have had trouble scratching himself let alone spelling his own name, decided to use my car for penalty practice, booting the door with a strong right foot.

What have I got myself into here? At four o'clock on a Monday afternoon, a friendly, lovely to see you in our country old boy would have been a pleasanter gesture than a karate kick to my car door. I didn't say anything offensive to this hooligan clown.

Yobbos are what the Aussies call them, but if the scenes from the last few days are any indication, our yobbos are more like Teletubbies in comparison. Indeed, there is nothing similar to this, in my experience, in Australia. Look out if Alan Shearer's header just misses the crossbar or Teddy Sheringham scores an own goal. Who will these hooligans take out their frustrations on then? A frightening thought.

As frightening is the subject of tooth extraction. A visit to the dentist, after dodging the hooligans on the High Street, confirmed my concern that my right eyetooth, smashed eight years ago by a Shane George bouncer, was finally dead and beyond reprieve. After two needles, the dentist used a horrendous metal extractor to tear my tooth slowly from its swollen and sore socket. The thought makes me cringe as I write.

He promised me it wouldn't hurt. He was right, but he did warn me that the extraction would sound and feel terrible. He knew what he was talking about. With mouth open wide, the procedure sounded like the crunching of walnuts with a nutcracker. He pulled the tooth one way, then the other, wiggled it from side to side and finally retrieved his target from my quivering mouth. Yuk!

After the bone-crunching extraction, I was wrong to think that the whole experience was over. The root was going to have to be dug out later. To cover the gaping hole, the dentist pushed a plastic plate and ceramic replacement tooth into place. Have you ever tried talking or eating with a clump of plastic stuck to the top of your hard palate? It's like having a plastic soap holder stuck to the top of your mouth. Sure it retains some dignity when I smile at my daughter, and it may stop me from looking like a convict, but when it comes to comfort and convenience, forget it.

A trip to the dentist is a most bizarre investment. You spend half an hour in complete discomfort and walk out with a numb face and a headache. A humbling experience. Let's face it, where else do you pay out your hard-earned cash for a session of torture and humiliation? Maybe some place in Soho, but I can't think of anywhere else!

On the way home from the dentist, and the hooligans, the rain still fell, the yobbos still snarled, my head still thumped and the Grand Canyon in my mouth still wept. I sat in my third traffic jam for the day and listened to the World Cup commentary. One thing's for sure – hooligans, dentists, traffic jams and more rain aren't my favourite things at the moment.

Tuesday, 16 June – living at Lord's and mental asylums

If nothing else, Lord's head groundsman Mick Hunt could never be accused of lacking dedication to his job. My spies tell me that Mick was up all last night keeping an eagle eye on his beloved Test match pitch. Come Thursday, Mick may be the most tired man in London. From all accounts he was awake until the sun came up this morning, drinking coffee and praying for the rain to hold off the sacred turf in his backyard.

Living in a small cottage on the Lord's premises, Mick doesn't have far to move from his bedroom to his office. It's not the worst backyard in the world, although if you were to ask Mick, who has been working at Lord's for over twenty years, he might tell you different.

His backyard may be one of the most famous in the world but at present it has its downside. With the extensive construction work being done to build the new, space-age media centre and grandstand, Mick's backyard hasn't exactly been the most peaceful of retreats over the last twelve months. The banging and crashing for every waking hour must be something of a headache for the Hunt family, and the working sites aren't exactly in the neat state that he keeps his ground and workshop.

Obviously preparations for the Test match pitch are currently Mick's highest priority and he will be leaving no stone unturned to produce the best possible surface for the all-important second Test. He and his willing workers have been literally working around the clock to produce the world-class pitch necessary to match all the other magic facilities of Lord's.

The little birdies have whispered to me that this pitch will have received as much tender loving care as any mummy's boy that I have ever known. Like a well-baked cake, the proof of Mick's dedication will be in the eating, or at least the playing, on the first morning of the second Test. There is no substitute for hard work in any profession and I am sure that although Mick will feel more like Mick Jagger after a bender come Thursday, the pitch will be a beauty.

Talk about ironies, the BBC news reported three rippers this afternoon. Firstly, I heard the weather forecast: 'Today will bring sunny spells and heavy rain.' Does that make sense? It's hardly a typical combination. Then there was the Supreme Court verdict on English au pair Louise Woodward, who was found to be 'still guilty but free to go home'. Strange! And finally, it was the conservationists' annual 'Keep Your Car at Home Day' but the public transport tube system just happened to be on strike, leaving egg on the face of a generally worthy campaign. It's a funny old world, isn't it?

While listening to the news in my car, Jamie Hewitt, my supposed navigator, and I got ourselves lost once again. A simple trip to Northampton turned into yet another epic disaster. Directions over the phone always sound so simple. To travel from Lord's to the Kookaburra factory in Corby, Northampton, my phone directions were as follows:

Mate, it's very easy. Take the M1 to junction 15,

which you follow until you see a sign for the A45. Drive along the A45, which turns into the A43 to Corby where you will drive past the salvage, spare parts car yard. Take a left on to the A14 through three roundabouts where you will see junction 7 and another large roundabout. Take the third exit on to the A6003, which is signposted Oakley Hay Industrial Estate, and follow it for three miles into the industrial estate. Then take your second turn right, and follow the street around to the end where you can't miss us.

It sounds fairly straightforward, and I thought it would be a breeze. Wrong! I should have learnt by now, never underestimate the distance between relevant signposts or the complexity of the English roundabouts, ring roads and dual carriageways. Thank goodness for mobile phones. Once again I arrived at my destination as a shaking lunatic, succumbing to the brutal frustrations of getting lost in the English road mazes. By the summer's end, I will either be the greatest cross-country driver and navigator in the UK, or doctors will meet me at Perth airport carrying straitjackets and tranquillisers. If I continue at this rate, the latter seems the more likely.

CHAPTER SEVEN

Lethal Weapons – Langer, Rose and Getz

Wednesday, 17 June – fast bowlers and more rain

Northamptonshire County Cricket Club is a very attractive cricket ground as far as cricket grounds go. The new, white indoor school acts as an over-accommodating sightscreen, the green trees to the right of the homely pavilion add a touch of nature and the old church steeple adds a touch of nostalgia to the playing arena. Add to these a lush green outfield and a flat brownish pitch and you have the makings of a most enjoyable day playing cricket.

The only problem with this lovely cricket setting is that the rain is falling . . . again. Like an annoying dripping tap, it is not pouring down but rather dribbling and spitting, making play today an impossibility. The scoreboard currently reads 'Inspection 12.45' but if I was a betting man I'd say the umpires will soon increase this prognosis to, at the very least, 'Inspection 2.30'.

It is funny being an opening batsman. Knowing that Northampton hosts the fast-bowling attack of Devon Malcolm, Franklyn Rose and David Follett, I don't know whether to laugh or cry in this situation. The more it rains, the more lively the pitch is likely to be, yet I suppose this rain is delaying the inevitable battle of wits between me as an opening batsman and Malcolm, Rose and Follett as nasty fast bowlers.

When you know you're playing these fast bowlers, it is amazing the demons which haunt your mind. You spend sleepless nights turning over evil thoughts of fire-breathing monsters with a blood-red leather projectile in their steel-clawed hands, conjuring up scenarios of deadly short balls tearing holes in your body, breaking arms and bruising you all over. Your mind should be sent to jail for laundering such useless thoughts.

Reality and common sense act as the good angels on your other shoulder, retaining sanity by reminding you that these monsters are really only human like you and me. Arriving at Northants, Devon beamed me a smile and shook my hand while Franklyn Rose, in his West Indian way, simply smiled, nodded and waved his big, gold-weighted hand.

People often ask me about facing fast bowling and I can honestly agree with Geoff Boycott who once said, 'Facing fast bowling is always worse the night before in your bed.' I think he is right. The only difference with facing the quicks, compared with a medium pacer or spinner, is that your feet have to move just a little quicker. If you watch the ball closely out of the hand, it is almost like slow motion because your mind has been programmed to do it naturally. The problem comes when you don't see it right out of the bowler's hand. It is then that you're in a bit more trouble, and those nightmares from the night before may suddenly turn to reality. This is an ugly time for any man, a time when you start to question the sense of opening the batting for a living.

As has become common this summer, the boys are trying everything to keep themselves occupied. Back in the changing-room, Phil Tufnell is passing the time dancing to *Saturday Night Fever*. The man moves like John Travolta, posing in front of the mirror wearing his tight suit pants, dark sunglasses, baseball cap turned backwards, and compulsory fag hanging out of his mouth. The London nightlife has taught him all the moves, and I must admit his jelly legs and Sinatra footwork are most impressive. If he had the same fancy feet with the bat in his hand, he may well have been the world's greatest all-rounder, both on and off the field.

With Tuffers continuing to jig, the rain continues to fall; the dripping tap has turned into a heavy shower. By the looks of the ground from our balcony, I'd say today may be yet another day described on Teletext as 'No play Wednesday due to rain'.

Thursday, 18 June – no play Thursday due to rain!

That is the all too familiar description on Ceefax. Surfing Ceefax, it quickly becomes clear that we are not the only fixture to have suffered from the continued grey skies and heavy, persistent rain. This weather is really becoming a pain in the backside.

At Lord's, although the start of the second Test was delayed until after lunch, Alec Stewart had no hesitation in asking the visitors to bat when he won his first toss of the series. Dominic Cork, the phoenix of English cricket, continued his successful comeback by taking the first four South African wickets.

With developing knowledge of my new home ground, it has become apparent that the ball swings around corners when the atmosphere is heavy with clouds. Seeing that the clouds were sitting above rather than floating over the grandpa pavilion, it was no surprise to see Cork and his bowling partners swinging the ball sharply away from the South African top order. A swinging ball is a dangerous ball to any batsman and with the clouds building, this Test could be a battle of technique and concentration against the talking Kookaburra ball.

As a matter of interest, I would like to have a look at the highlights of Bob Massie's famous Test match debut in 1972. I would be very surprised to see a clear sky when Massie produced those marvellous spells of swing bowling.

It is fascinating to observe the change in the momentum of the game when the atmosphere alters. Almost like magic, the ball tends to stop swinging as soon as the skies clear. With a better forecast for the rest of this week, England would have been a little disappointed to have let their opponents off the hook in the last hour and a half of play. Jonty Rhodes, batting positively, and captain Hansie Cronje fought confidently to save their team from a disaster.

You just never know what's around the corner in this game. Only a few weeks ago, I sat on the tube with Jonty and sensed a grim feeling regarding his personal prospects for the remainder of this tour. He is now on the verge of a Test century, a century that three weeks ago seemed so far out of reach. During our short chat on the tube, he was fairly convinced that his tour may have been over barring an injury to one of his team-mates. Recognised throughout his career as a one-day specialist, Jonty was of the opinion that, as the one-day series was over, he may be spending a long summer carrying the drinks and occasionally showing off his brilliant fielding skills. It is amazing how quickly things change around and it is a tribute to the little dynamo's work ethic and determination that he is now cemented in the Test team. His positive footwork and aggressive running between the wickets make him a very valuable middle-order Test batsman and, of course, his fielding speaks for itself. He could finish this series as one of the key members of his team; not a bad turnaround from the twelfth-man duties he was half expecting a few weeks ago.

Only thirty-four overs were bowled on the first day of this second Test – a great shame for the players and crowd who cherish day one of the Lord's Test. It is particularly disappointing for Steve James, the prolific Glamorgan opening batsman, who gained his just reward and his first Test cap for his consistent run-scoring as an opening batsman in county cricket. It is always great to see players like James earning a reward for their outstanding performances. No doubt he would have sighed a breath of relief when his skipper sent the opposition into bat. It is always nice to get a feel for the game by spending some time fielding before facing the fire in your debut Test. It would be encouraging to see this consistent performer in county cricket take his dedication and ability to the next level by performing well in this Test series. Anyone who scores as many runs as he has deserves every opportunity that is granted to him.

Friday, 19 June – getting a bowl

You know how kids beg their mums for an ice-cream or a chocolate bar in a supermarket? Well, like one of those nagging little kids I have been reduced to begging Ramps or Browny for a bowl ever since arriving in England. Until today my efforts have been futile. Both captains have just smiled politely, shaking their heads as if to say, 'Please don't embarrass me. How can I possibly let a pie-thrower like you bowl in first-class cricket? All that it will do is bring the game into disrepute.'

Now I will be the first to admit I haven't got the perfect Imran Khan action. I don't get the bounce of Curtly Ambrose or the reverse swing of Waqar Younis. In fact, I will even admit that I look like your perfect Peter Pie-thrower when delivering the cricket ball. But aesthetics apart, I also know that if I put enough balls in the right spot, swing it a little bit this way and that, and get a few to stay a bit low, I can do a job for the boys.

I have tried all the lines: 'Trust me, I take wickets in club cricket back home' and 'What have we got to lose at this stage?' even, 'I promise they come out better than they look'. Every one of them has just been knocked back by my smiling, disbelieving skipper. That is, until today.

The over before tea, Browny finally succumbed to my relentless pleas and pseudo warm-up actions in the field, and threw me the ball. 'Go on Alfy, [after Allan 'Alfie' Langer, the famous Australian rugby league player] have a go. Let's have a look at what you've got.'

Obviously having an eye for talent, Browny must

It was while on tour with Australia during the 1997 Ashes series that I was approached about playing for Middlesex the following season – I jumped at the chance. Here I'm jumping against Mark Taylor, testing out our Aussie Rules technique. (*Philip Brown*)

(ABOVE) Preparing for an innings in the AXA Sunday League, and raring to go. Meanwhile, Phil Tufnell (BELOW) has a slightly different way of psyching himself up. (*Richard Johnson*)

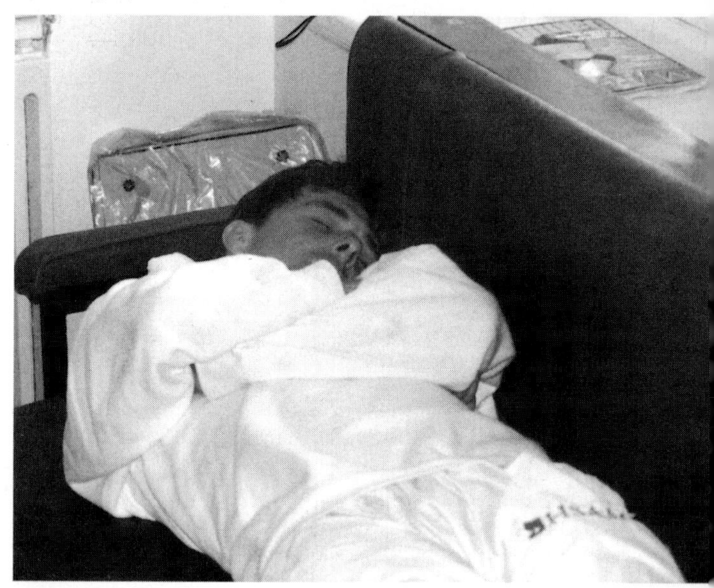

The changing-rooms at Lord's are incredible – loads of space, cushioned benches, tea and coffee. However, good as they are, I'd always rather be out in the middle. (*Richard Johnson*)

Saluting my first century at Lord's, the Mecca of cricket, on 15 May against Somerset, which came as a relief in case the Middlesex members were wondering about their overseas signing. I went on to make 233 not out, and we won the match. My partner David Nash made his first century that day too. (*Richard Johnson*)

The celebrations continued in the field, but unfortunately we didn't have as many as we would have liked during the season. (*Philip Brown*)

John Buchanan, the Middlesex coach, is a great success in Australia but he found it more difficult to implement his methods in England. (*Philip Brown*)

The county brains trust: Mr Middlesex Mike Gatting, captain Mark Ramprakash, vice-captain Keith Brown, John Buchanan and physio Simon Shephard. (*Richard Johnson*)

When Mike Gatting and I reached 368 for our opening partnership against Essex at Southgate we broke the county record – it was a wonderful day batting with one of the county's all-time greats. (*PA*)

Afterwards we decided to have a photo taken to record the moment – definitely one for the family album! (*Philip Brown*)

Mark Ramprakash had a difficult first full season in charge of the county. But he has a good young squad, and the future prospects are looking bright. (*Richard Johnson*)

I wasn't really waving to the camera! (*Philip Brown*)

Batting at Lord's – perhaps the greatest thrill for me as an Australian visitor. The opportunity helped make the season a tremendous experience. (*Craig Prentis/Allsport*)

have been at least semi-impressed as he threw me the ball for a couple of overs after the break. Five overs, and figures of one for ten later, I was asked to take a spell. How pumped do you think I was!

A little inswinger down the leg side gave Browny a stumping and me my first wicket in county cricket. Yes! Having bet Jamie Hewitt fifty quid at the start of the season that I would take ten championship wickets for the season, I am now on my way. Ten wickets is quite a few for a bowler of my lack of ability but you just never know.

The way I see it, all I have to do is keep bugging my captain, like that persistent little child, until he can no longer put up with the pressure. I figure he will eventually get sick of my begging and surrender, just like the mum who eventually surrenders and lets her kid have that chocolate bar or ice-cream. If today is anything to go by, all I need is continued persistence and nine more unfortunate county batsmen to help me over the line.

Having read all season about Northants batsman Malachy Loye it was good to see him in action first hand today. Any player who scores 300 in an innings must be a class act and we weren't to be disappointed. A natural-looking player who hits the ball cleanly, I wouldn't be surprised to see him progress through the ranks and push for higher honours. Like many young English players, he hits the ball very hard and looks technically correct. If he continues to post big hundreds he should be recognised before long.

Another young player impressing at present is tear-away fast bowler Tim Bloomfield. He bowls fast, aggressive outswingers and although he has some work to do on his fitness, I think he is another fine prospect. From ten first-class games he has taken three five-wicket hauls. This is a remarkable feat from this raw young man, who drives a delivery truck in the winter.

Today he could have taken six wickets had it not been for an unfortunate incident in the closing moments. When Devon Malcolm came into bat, Northants had two overs and two balls remaining before stumps. The rules state that if the final batsman is out with more than two overs remaining, the fielding side will have to go in to bat for one over before stumps. As an opener there is nothing worse than this; in fact, it is a cricket nightmare.

As Devon walked in to bat, I jokingly asked Tim to bowl wide of the stumps or at least a little slower to allow Devon a chance of survival for two balls. We had a laugh about it and Tim, who was fired up and bowling well, simply smiled and walked back to his mark. The first ball was fast and straight and Devon played it with a remarkably straight bat, surviving the golden duck. Only one ball to go and we were safe until tomorrow.

With six wickets on offer, 'Bloomers' bowled another fast outswinger which Devon swung at like a maniac in a pub brawl. Not collecting it as he would have liked, the ball lobbed up to David Nash at gully. In describing this catch we are talking about an absolute sitter but much to everyone's astonishment, Nashy juggled it like a piece of wet soap before watching it fall safely to the ground.

With the soap lying on the grass, all hell broke loose. Fiery at the best of times, Bloomers gave Nashy the fast-bowler's stare, which is as bad as that look from your grade-three teacher. Looking for somewhere to disappear is impossible on a cricket field where there is plenty of space to run, but nowhere to hide.

The dropped catch may have ensured us a night's reprieve, but poor old Nashy had to survive an even worse ordeal for the remainder of the afternoon. A Tim Bloomfield abuse session is not a pretty sight and I am sure if Nashy had been given a choice he would have taken an over of batting any time.

Saturday, 20 June – bargaining and negotiating, contrived results and hooking West Indians

I have never seen anything like it. Like bargain hunters in a Hong Kong flea market, captains Brown and Curran haggled with each other for every single run, every single over, and every single con trick they could muster. They weren't doing it to take a few pence off a pound of carrots or a skinny chicken, but rather to gain some advantage for their respective teams.

So much for just playing cricket, I thought to myself as the haggling almost became a comedy show.

Firstly, Northants skipper Kevin Curran suggested that we forfeit our first innings and chase the 363 runs that they scored when they batted. In ninety-four overs he considered this to be a fair run-chase. Unfortunately, it was a fair equation in his mind but an unfair one in ours. Considering we would have fewer overs to bat than they had, and keeping in mind that they hosted an international attack, Browny left the first round of negotiations shaking his head.

As in any negotiation, it was up to Keith Brown, our captain, to go back with a counter-offer. Having discussed the prospects with his team-mates last night, and again this morning, he went back to the table and asked politely for a target of 300 in eighty-two overs. Northants quickly dismissed this as being a ludicrous target, but they would be willing to set 330 in eighty-two overs.

From round two, the negotiations became incredible. You could have mistaken the atmosphere for a negotiation between President Clinton and Saddam Hussein, such was the determination of each leader. For half an hour, both captains almost begged each other for an extra five or ten runs' leniency while the overs were juggled between eighty-five and ninety.

Here we had an unfortunate situation resulting from two abandoned days of play. The captains were attempting to squeeze an outright result out of two days of cricket. It is a situation I have never experienced before, as contrived results have been outlawed in Sheffield Shield cricket in Australia. Five minutes before the final day of play was to due to get under way, I was waiting in the changing-room with my opening partner, Richard Kettleborough. Sitting in our creams, we were both unsure whether we were about to face the fire of one of the best fast-bowling attacks in the country, or whether we were about to score the easiest first-class runs of our lives. Were we supposed to dress up in thigh guards, arm guards and helmets, for an assault from Malcolm, Rose and Follett, or was the more appropriate attire caps and sunglasses for a four-over slog to make up the negotiated equation?

As the clock ticked closer to the start, more unexpected rain began to fall giving the captains a little extra time for discussion, a discussion which had transmuted many times. Eventually, an agreeable equation was reached that relied upon Northants giving us 80 runs in four overs (yes, that is 20 runs an over). When this was achieved, we agreed to declare, then they would declare their second innings at 0 for 0, leaving us a chase of 280, in fifty-four overs.

I had heard about it before, even seen it on television, but actually playing in a set-up game was certainly different. The first 80 were a breeze; I wish opening the batting always proved as fruitful. In three point three overs, twenty-one balls, or more accurately twenty-one lobbed full tosses, we had reduced the margin to the agreed 280 and the game was set.

It is a shame the game ever has to be lowered to this. Understandably the weather in England doesn't help matters, but still, playing the game like this, even if it is only for fifteen minutes and three point three overs to set up a more lucrative result, is a shame in my eyes. From all accounts, this happened more often in the days of three-day county matches. I am glad I wasn't around then, although it would have done wonders for my batting average.

Facing slow full tosses is hardly the ideal preparation for what was to follow. Devon Malcolm and Franklyn Rose are two of the world's quickest bowlers, and with a sniff of victory, they can become quite ugly bowlers from twenty-two yards away. When you are standing at one end with a bat in your hand and they have a brand new cricket ball in their claw, the game becomes more like a heavyweight boxing fight than the gentlemanly game of cricket that it is supposed to be.

After seeing off the first three overs and pushing

my score along to 3, with three singles, Franklyn Rose commenced his second over from the Members' End. The first three balls he launched at me were fast inswingers that hit me on the left pad, my inside thigh guard and my right foot. This huge West Indian, with more gold than Mr T, really meant business and he had me jumping around like a jack-in-the-box.

As he sprinted in for his fourth ball, I continued my normal routine: eyes around, get your feet moving, and most importantly, watch the ball, see it out of his hand. Obviously one part of this routine mantra went wrong because as he let go of the ball I thought I saw it early and my body got itself into a position to hook.

I was sure it was there to hook!

Instinctively I realised, a little too late, that this one was a bit quicker than the others he had bowled to me. As a result of my late movement I was left sitting on my backside, seeing stars and clenching my left temple, which felt like it was going to explode and send my brain somewhere towards Mars.

Now I have been hit on the helmet many times before – I guess it is one of the perks of being a top-order batsman – but this time it was different and even a little scary. As I stood up, my mind was in frenzy. Automatically I started thinking about my daughter, my wife, my family back in Australia and my younger days. It was almost like I was in the *X-Files* and I was about to be banished to outer space for my troubles. The ball must have hit me right in the wrong place, a little closer for comfort than you would generally like.

A visit to the local hospital and an X-ray of my skull

revealed nothing abnormal, except a big bullseye target, offering any West Indian bowler at least one free shot at my skull per innings. This seems to be the trend. These West Indian pacemen have a habit of hitting me on the helmet. At times I wish I could return the favour but from five foot eight I know this is only a wishful and happy dream.

Retired hurt 3, a quickfire 50 from about fourteen balls, a drawn match and my first county wicket – this was a disappointing result to a disappointing game marred by rain, changing-room squabbling about run rates and contrived results.

These contrived results are surely not healthy for the game, although if it allows the players and spectators to obtain more satisfaction from the county game then I concede they are a necessity. Anything to produce positive, live, first-class cricket must be encouraged even if a few minutes of joke cricket has to be tolerated.

Sunday, 21 June – drive-through restaurants

Leo Getz, à la Joe Pesci in *Lethal Weapon, Two, Three,* and *Four* sums it up perfectly: 'They always get you at the drive-through. They always get it wrong, because they know you won't be bothered turning around and going all the way back to get it right. They always get you, it is a fact of life and I hate that,' he screams from the back seat of the car. He admittedly uses stronger language to make his point to his buddies, detectives Riggs (Mel Gibson) and Murtaugh (Danny Glover), but he hits the nail right on the head.

Driving back from Northampton tonight after a disappointing day and with my family up in Scotland, the prospect of arriving home to an empty London flat prompted me to call in for a takeaway hamburger.

After ordering a burger and a fillet of fish from the friendly young girl in the orders booth, I paid my money and drove back on to the motorway to head home. Two hundred metres down the busy London road, I reached into my bag of goodies and, with clever manipulation, managed to take the fillet of fish out of its plastic container before taking a big bite out of my evening's dinner. As in the scene from *Lethal Weapon*, you can't understand how upset I was when out of the tender hundred per cent cod, as it was described on the menu board, a dollop of cold syrup spurted into the back of my throat. It was still half frozen. Yuk! They had done me, just like Leo had said they would.

In disgust I threw the fish back into the paper bag, knowing that my burger was sure to offer me more delight. Wrong again. The edges of the bread roll were like cardboard, all hard and chewy, while the hamburger patties were cold and 'orrible as my London team-mates would say. Sure I thought about turning around and going back to give them a blast, but, like Leo predicted, I couldn't really be bothered, after just driving an hour and a half from Northampton.

It had been a long enough day as it was and the last thing I felt like doing was going back to the smiling cashier to vent my anger. Already it was late at night and although I was hungry, my bed was calling me from another ten miles away. They had got me, I should have listened to a friendly piece of Hollywood advice. Maybe I'll know better next time, but then again, I am sure it won't be the last time I get ripped off by a fast-food, drive-through restaurant.

Back to cricket and England collapsed terribly this afternoon to lose the second Test against South Africa. When I went out to bat for Middlesex at 2.00 p.m. England were cruising at 213 for 3 with Nasser Hussain and Alec Stewart batting very comfortably. By 3.30, I had to look twice at the Test match update on the Northampton scoreboard, which read England 232 for 7.

The press will no doubt report today's collapse as an all too familiar scene for English cricket. Just as it seems that England are fighting back, disaster seems to strike. The frightening part of today's loss is that the South Africans won it without extraordinary contributions from Allan Donald or Shaun Pollock, the two men who generally play the role as the visitors' main destroyers. Jacques Kallis and Lance Klusener are both very good bowlers, but they are not generally the guys who ruin a team's ambition and spirit like they have done in this second innings.

Today will be a massive body blow to England's confidence and spirit. Not only have they gone one-nil down in the series but they nearly lost the services of Mark Ramprakash for the next Test match. The one-match suspended sentence, for showing dissent, seems very harsh and my heart is really going out to Ramps tonight. Knowing how hard he has worked to cement his place in the Test team, his world would have been shattered had the referee gone one step further in his verdict.

It will take a lot of character for the hosts to fight back from here. As South Africa celebrate tonight in the West End, England will be sitting back wondering how they are going to find an answer to this world-class bowling attack.

Monday, 22 June – the pressure of Test cricket

What did Mark Ramprakash say to senior Australian umpire Darrell Hair at Lord's on Saturday? Whatever it was, it cost him a substantial fine, a suspended one-match ban and perhaps most disappointingly a black mark on his strong and very likeable character.

The hefty fine and a six-month suspended sentence would suggest that the words he used were very heated and pointed towards the umpire. Even the close-up cameras that followed Ramps off the field showed some muttering, but it was impossible to figure exactly what he said. We all know that lip reading is usually pretty easy when the cameras are right up on a sportsman's face but in Ramps' case even the most astute lip readers must have struggled to decipher what was said.

Today at Lord's I asked Ramps exactly what he did say and I must admit I was surprised that the seven words he used could land him in such hot water. 'Darrell, you are messing with my career' were the dreaded seven words. Hardly the ferocious attack that many people watching the replays may have expected. It would have been easy for all of us to jump to the conclusion that his reaction was fiercer, as the severity of the penalty suggested.

Showing dissent, whether in the form of physical dissent, i.e. standing at the crease for too long, showing your disappointment, or anger, at an umpire's decision, or verbal dissent, i.e. saying something towards the umpire, is definitely taboo in the modern game of cricket. In this world of modern communications, specifically video cameras and replays, the players and umpires are under the most intense scrutiny every time they are on the field of play. The ICC (International Cricket Committee) have made it very clear that any behaviour not befitting a professional cricketer will very quickly be stamped out of the game. On this occasion, Ramps was the player who copped the penalty for his show of dissent, or more specifically, his show of disappointment.

After batting heroically for his sinking team, he was given out caught behind off what he, the commentators and the general public all agreed was a tough decision. After standing at the crease for two seconds, he walked past Darrell Hair, who is an excellent umpire and a good bloke, before muttering his passionate words.

Now Ramps would never condone any behaviour that would bring the game into disrepute. He is a man of strong will and determination, a true professional who plays the game with all his heart and soul. Sometimes his character may land him in hot water as it did in this situation. His seven words were a heat-of-the-moment reaction, and if cameras hadn't been present at the ground scrutinising his every breath and step, I'm sure no one would ever have realised that there was an incident.

Players, like umpires, are under enormous pressure in the Test arena. A rough decision in the first innings, followed by a good ball in the second, can suddenly put a batsman's position in the team in doubt. A player like Ramps plays the game with great passion as it is; he is desperate to prove himself at the highest level. On top of the personal pride and desire, there is the pressure of the team performance, as well as the substantial financial incentives offered for, and relying upon, success.

With this in mind, people should understand that the

human emotion of disappointment is likely to show its face in certain circumstances. It is disappointing that my Middlesex captain has been penalised for his actions; I know he will take it on the chin. I hope people never lose sight of the fact that this game is played by human beings who are likely to show their emotions and make mistakes. This to me is the allure of sport; the way people react to the highs and lows of the game reflects character.

Umpires are human too; they are as likely to make mistakes as anyone. Their job is as cutthroat as the players they officiate. Their margin for error is now nil. With such close scrutiny of every single delivery bowled in a match, an umpire has to observe every ball under incredible pressure. There is no longer the concept of a close decision because on nine out of ten occasions the video will show up what the human eye could never see. In this era it is either in or out, just ask the video.

Test cricket is big business with the financial rewards for both players and umpires substantial. Anyone who thinks the people involved in Test cricket are too highly paid should look very closely at the pressure they are subjected to every time they take the field.

Rub out bad sportsmanship and get rid of the yobbos who bring the game into disrepute, but never eliminate the emotions involved in the game. Don't breed robots; instead, encourage the characters and feelings of the game. Sympathise with the players and umpires before knocking them down, which is easier to do now because of the marvellous, but at times dangerous, modern technology. There is more at the heart of the game we love than just the statistics and physical process of bat on ball. Let's enjoy that and never forget it.

CHAPTER EIGHT
Searching for the Winning Habit

Tuesday, 23 June – London parking

Finding a car spot in London is as frustrating as trying to find a dropped contact lens in the middle of the night. It can be an ordeal similar to eating a chilli hot dog before boarding a roller-coaster ride. Inevitably it makes you sick, especially on those occasions when you are in some sort of hurry or there's some urgency in reaching your destination. With this in mind, I had to laugh at my wife's solution to road rage this morning.

Before starting with this story, a little history should be provided.

After dropping me at Southgate Cricket Club yesterday, Sue found herself stuck on the North Circular road in a sixty-minute traffic jam. With Jessica screaming her lungs out in her abhorred car seat, already late for her bottle and morning sleep and hating every minute of this seven-mile, eighty-minute drive home, the atmosphere in the Langer car wasn't particularly relaxed. To top it off, the rain was as heavy as a weight-watchers drop-out, leaving Sue, understandably, at the end of her tether as she finally reached our West Hampstead street. Driving up the road, she watched like a desperate eagle, hoping, even praying, that she might get lucky and find that elusive car-parking spot.

Unfortunately, the only available space on this treacherous Monday morning was one that had been reserved by three orange witch's hats, presumably for a disabled driver, a council chore, or some other fair cause. Not unusually, the lack of spaces meant that Sue missed out on a space in the street, leaving her with no other option than to park three parallel streets away. This in itself is a pain in the backside, but when you are five months' pregnant and have to run with a screaming child in your arms, without an umbrella, in the pouring rain, the pain becomes more than a hangover headache.

Arriving home soaking wet, Sue eventually settled Jessica to sleep and sat down for a well-earned cup of tea. She stared out of the bay window, reflecting on the morning chaos and meditating on the continued heavy rain.

After a couple of sips of her tea, my generally philosophical and calm wife sat up in her armchair and flew into her second rage for the day. The carefully laid out orange cones were being removed, not by the imagined council worker or disabled parker, but by a scruffy-looking resident of the street. On pulling up beside the orange markers in his van, he placed the witch's hats in the back of his vehicle, looked around sheepishly and briskly retreated into his flat. This same fully mobile resident, who normally parks in the space marked 'disabled', obviously figured he was well within his rights to save a spot right outside his flat. In her anger and disbelief, Sue sat down and penned a note of disgust intended to go under his windscreen wiper:

'You are a very rude man. We are all at a disadvantage with the lack of parking at our homes; however your behaviour is completely selfish. You are not disabled, however you park in a disabled permit zone. Then when that spot is unavailable, you have the nerve to put witch's hats out to save yourself another spot.

'Next time, the hats will be removed so that another resident, especially those with children, will have a chance. How about considering somebody besides yourself for once?'

After cooling down to her normal sane self, Sue decided that her behaviour was probably a little childish and motivated mainly by her own bad day on the North Circular. After putting it into perspective she decided to let it go, probably too scared to be caught placing her grievances under the bloke's windscreen wiper, if the truth be known.

So that is the history of the road-raged wife.

It wasn't until this morning that I had to laugh, when Sue looked out of our bay window only to see the three orange cones once again placed neatly in the spare space across the road.

'Enough is enough,' she cried, 'do you dare me to go and move them?'

A little smile appeared on my disbelieving face as she donned one of my big black coats, a pair of dark Oakley sunglasses and tucked her long hair up into a dark cap. Looking quite the suspicious villain she slammed the front door and stomped up the street pretending to be a man on a mission.

As I hid behind the heavy curtains covering the bay window, my hesitant grin slowly turned into schoolboy giggles and then raucous laughter. There, before my very eyes, my incognito wife threw the orange cones, one by one, without regard, on to the footpath, freeing up the space for someone more deserving, in her mind. It was like a scene from a Hollywood movie. With that she marched back down the street, hid behind a car, took off the jacket and sunnies and pulled her hair out so that she now looked like a pregnant young mother rather than a mafia hit man. Back up the street she sauntered, smiling like a naughty schoolkid, obviously delighted with her little masquerade.

On returning to the flat, she sat at the window and cheered like an English football fan after a World Cup goal when another car pulled into the sacred space. With mission half accomplished, she waited for the culpable van to return home to its sacred stable. When he finally arrived, we watched him excitedly as he shook his head, leapt out of his van and retrieved his scattered witch's hats from the verge before driving away like a Formula One car driver. With this, Sue started running around the flat like an excited three-year-old, offering me high fives, delighted that her Good Samaritan act had paid off.

A couple of hours later, Sue's adrenalin levels were still up and noticing that the van had once again found its way back to a position outside the opposite flat, she decided to finish off the groggy opponent. She re-dressed like mafioso Sam 'Mooney' Giancana and crept up behind all the other parked cars before leaving her penned note underneath the windscreen wiper. This time she returned with her heart beating like a stopwatch, nervous, but obviously chuffed at her day's achievement – an unbelievable performance from my wife, generally so sensible, showing that there is a little road-rage Robin Hood in all of us.

Saturday, 27 June – Mr Middlesex

Red wine is one of his favoured hobbies and like a 1955 bottle of Penfolds Grange Hermitage, Mike Gatting showed today that he is also improving with age. Gatt is like one of the antique chairs that sit in the Long Room at Lord's. Not only is he reliable and sturdy like the old, solid-oak chair but he just seems to be part of the furniture of Middlesex and English cricket.

Although he has trouble facing blond leg-spinners who turn the ball sharply from outside leg stump to off (who doesn't?), and although he once played one reverse sweep too many, he really has achieved everything there is to achieve in this great game. Tonight he is 180 not out and, if I say so myself, 180 of the best runs you are likely to see.

For me, his innings at Southgate today draws parallels with England football coach Glenn Hoddle. Only last night Hoddle had a dig at those critics in the media who have criticised him for a number of his tactics in the qualifying round of the World Cup. After their inspiring victory against Colombia, Hoddle reminded the English press, and public, about Darren Anderton's first-up goal. For the last week the press have been on his back about selecting Anderton ahead of David Beckham. 'Hoddle is out of his mind' the press screamed. 'Hoddle couldn't tie his own shoelaces, let alone coach our football team' another mocked. Now, after an inspired victory, and a brilliant game for Anderton, his critics seemed to have been silenced, for the short term anyway, and oh didn't he enjoy that!

While it took Gatt a little longer than ninety minutes to silence his critics and bring up his ninety-third first-class century, I am sure he'll be feeling equally chuffed tonight as he recalls a few of the criticisms of the past few months. As is his way, Gatt used his bat to do all his talking, probably the only way to do it.

Since arriving in England, I have listened to, and read about, all the reasons why Mike Gatting should have retired from the game. Cricket has been his life for well over two decades! Before meeting Mike Gatting as a team-mate, the critics' points of view made some sense. He is forty-one, he may be a little slower in the field and he now has other roles to play within English cricket, e.g. as a national selector. After three months of sitting in the changing-room with Mr Middlesex, I can see that all of that may be true but I can also see that his so-called limitations quickly fade into irrelevance. From a team point of view, he is an invaluable member of the current Middlesex County Cricket Club team. Without exception, he still works as hard as anyone in the team, his technique is outstanding and he obviously has a great love and passion for the game of cricket.

Opening the innings with Gatt has been a great experience, with today being the highlight of an enjoyable combination. In surpassing the highest first-wicket partnership (of 367) for Middlesex, I have to say I had a most enjoyable seven hours with the old master.

No matter what situation presented itself, Gatt always seemed to have an answer. For seven hours it felt like I was the student. While we played, we talked about the game, and enjoyed the experience of feeling in total control of the opposition.

Being fifteen years my senior, the running between wickets wasn't exactly like a Jonty Rhodes/Michael Bevan partnership but I have to say the old fella is very competitive and he was always ready for even the shortest of singles. What he lacks in raw speed he makes up in gutsy determination and stamina. As we walked off the ground together this afternoon, he looked as fresh as a sprouting daisy. My legs were aching, he looked as though he had just spent the day at a health farm. How he does it is beyond me.

I am often asked what we talk about for seven hours together at the crease. For me batting is about improving with every venture to the crease, so when I get the opportunity to bat with someone like Gatt I try to draw as much information from him as I possibly can.

Today, I asked him about what the best way to play the offspinner, Peter Such, would be when he has set quite defensive fields. His answer to that was to suggest I keep milking him, in other words look for the few gaps, stay patient and make him come to me rather than me get frustrated and give him my wicket. He also hammered into me that it is worth cashing in on days like this because there are plenty of times when you get out early.

The old master also helped me when I started to feel tired. 'Keep chewing that gum, master,' he kept repeating every time I started to get lazy. In other words stay focused, stay with me mate, and be determined not to give them an inch. 'Keep chewing that gum master, keep chewing that gum', over and over like a mantra.

Admittedly, all the time isn't spent on cricket. Believe it or not we were having a lot of fun out there today. It was the two of us versus eleven of them and we were having a fantastic time. After a while we started to relax and the conversation turned briefly to red wine, the beautiful Southgate ground, the struggling Essex fieldsmen and the kids running around the marquees. We both know the importance of staying relaxed at the crease so we just kept each other smiling and focused. 'Beware the smiling assassins' is a quote I swear by in the game of cricket. A smiling relaxed player is the toughest opponent as it generally means they are at ease with the world as we were during our partnership.

Gatt says that this is definitely his last county season. He has seven centuries to go to reach the esteemed mark of a hundred first-class centuries, a milestone that must be acting as a carrot for the man who really has achieved everything there is to achieve in his distinguished career. Before today, I had the feeling that even Gatt, as proud as he is, was starting to feel that the one hundred hundreds feat was nearly beyond him. The carrot was diminishing in size and Mount Everest was starting to look invincible. Knowing Gatt, I get the feeling that while he is drinking his pint of lager tonight he might just rethink his ambitions. Suddenly the fire may be re-ignited. After hitting every ball in the middle of his bat, I think the target may suddenly seem more realistic. As so often happens in sport, the tables can change with the blink of an eye, or in this case the flash of a bat.

Personally, I would love to see him achieve the

prestigious target. Not many men have given as much to the game as Mike Gatting has to English cricket and I feel it would be only just that he achieves this final honour. If nothing else, I hope when he does decide that it's time to hang up his boots he will make the decision to retire of his own accord, not as a result of other people's opinions or speculations. For now, though, I just hope Gatt continues to teach me more about the intricacies of county cricket. Whether it is the joy of batting in long partnerships, the pleasure of bacon sandwiches for breakfast or a few shared bottles of red wine, Mike Gatting is an outstanding bloke to have on your side.

Sunday, 28 June – it should have been us

We needed just four wickets after tea to defeat Essex outright, but we had to settle for a closely fought draw. I might be getting a little carried away but this result is really disappointing for me. It almost seemed as though our guys were happy that we didn't lose the game rather than disappointed that we didn't win when we should have done. Maybe it is just a different attitude I have to playing the game of cricket. In Australia we tend to play to win, even if that means risking defeat. At times I feel we are playing to avoid defeat rather than nailing a victory. At the end of the day, championships are won by gaining maximum points as many times as possible during the season. Drawn matches will add up to a middle of the table result of mediocrity, which is not really why you play the game in my view.

We should have bowled out the Essex tail today.

Instead we were a little too defensive in our approach, giving the opposition a chance to stay in the game and even win it in the end. Attitude plays such an important role in success. In batting, there is a difference between batting to score runs and batting not to get out, just as there is a difference between playing to win and playing not to lose. It seems that English cricket often revolves around playing not to lose rather than going all out to win. In my view this is a dangerous and negative approach that is sure to have less successful ramifications than a more positive and aggressive style of competing.

Tuesday, 30 June – a football yobbo for one night!

After travelling up the motorway again this afternoon, we checked into our Nottinghamshire hotel to be greeted by a mass of red and white banners and streamers, and signs everywhere announcing live coverage on the big screen of tonight's World Cup clash. Never have I seen so much excitement and expectation in one hotel foyer. Checking in is usually a bit of a drag but my Middlesex team-mates and the hotel staff didn't seem to be in any hurry today; they all chatted merrily about England's prospects for the big second-round game against Argentina. From all the hype, I knew tonight was an enormous occasion for every proud pommy football fan.

Come to think about it, this means about ninety-eight per cent of England.

* * *

When the whistle blew and the game kicked off, it was as though the tension had finally been relieved. The hotel bar was full of fans who had come from far and wide to see their boys on the big screen. Dressed in wigs and football shirts, skulling pints of Tetley bitter and smoking cigarettes, the supporters were out in force. Because the view for a short arse like myself was hindered by the bewigged football lovers in the bar, my mates and I decided to retreat to Phil Tufnell's room for a far better view of the game. Sitting in Tuffers' hotel room with my Middlesex team-mates, the atmosphere watching the match was electric, as I am sure it was in most pubs, lounge-rooms, bedrooms and clubs around England. I imagine every venue offering television access had patriotic fans singing, shouting, moaning, groaning and eventually crying at the brave England fight for World Cup survival. Room 211 could have been mistaken for front-row seats at the actual game in St Etienne, such was the noise being generated by my pumped-up buddies. Rather than escaping the bedlam from the bar, the scenes in room 211 were equally thunderous.

When Michael Owen, the little genius from Liverpool, won a penalty and Alan Shearer scored the first goal to equalise, the room was filled with total pandemonium. The atmosphere was even more electric when Owen's brilliant solo effort put England in the lead, which was equalised by Argentina just before half-time. Then Sol Campbell headed a corner ball into the back of the net, putting England ahead and sending 211 into a state of total euphoria. As the ball hit the net, Tuffers bounced up from his seat, dropped his fag and grabbed Keith Dutch who was already hugging Gatt who had instantly grabbed Richard Johnson who was kissing David Nash. Before you knew it, there were ten jubilant Middlesex cricketers embracing each other on the bed and jumping around like it was a scene from a Greek orgy.

As if a dose of VD had struck the orgy scene, the ten passionate huggers instantly disbanded when the referee disallowed the goal. Disappointment quickly turned into disbelief as the ref's decision left the Argentinian players running riot in the midfield; they converged upon David Seaman's goalmouth like a pack of hungry dogs. The ref's call caused all sorts of embarrassment in room 211 as the boys had to take back their emotional hugs, kisses and passionate embraces before spending the final minutes berating the man in black, the coach and, of course, David Beckham.

Bottles of Foster's Light Ice had to be used to prevent the carpet, smouldering from Tuffers' dropped cigarette, from bursting into flames. Had the goal been allowed the hotel may have burnt to the ground – I am sure a few flames wouldn't have distracted the celebrations. From my point of view, the fire extinguishing came as something of a relief; for a few quiet moments, the energy was taken away from the game. With everyone in the room having an opinion on the state of play and the way England should be going about their business, it was opportune to have the focus diverted, even if it was to stop another fire.

The biggest moment of debate was when David Beckham was sent off moments into the second half. I don't know much about football, but even I thought it was a pretty dumb thing for him to do. As it turned out, it may have been a telling factor in the final result and unsurprisingly was almost as big news as the sinking of the *Titanic*. No one died as a result of Beckham's misdemeanour, but the effect on the whole of England was almost as emotional and melodramatic. Talkback shows were calling for the reinstatement of capital punishment, while the newspapers were treating Beckham with the same respect as they might grant a serial killer. From David Beckham's point of view, it was a horrendous error of judgement.

Tonight, for a few moments, I felt what it must be like to be a football yobbo or a member of the Barmy Army. It is so easy from the other side of the fence where the only pressure comes from how many opinions you can have every thirty minutes and how much louder you can sing or shout than your mate beside you. I really had a great night. The only problem is that, as England lost on penalties, none of us will be able to do it all again on Saturday night with the boys. England are out of the World Cup and the country is in mourning as, once again, England will be described as heroes in defeat. As Tuffers put it, 'Big deal. The fact is we have lost again. Heroes in defeat, that means bugger all. You can't bring home the World Cup if you're not even in the quarter-finals, can you?'

This summed up the feelings in the dejected room 211 on World Cup knock-out night.

CHAPTER NINE

From Tests to Village Greens

Wednesday, 1 July – just plain ugly

I have seen some shockers in my time but I have never seen anything like this! It was hideous to look at and yet it played well. The old cliché about judging the book, or in this case the pitch, by its cover rang true this morning when we arrived at Trent Bridge.

When arriving at a new fixture, the routine first stop for any pro cricketer is the centre square. Before you even sip your first mandatory cup of tea or coffee, the urge to view the groundsman's finished product drags you from the changing-room like a staple is drawn to a magnet. We all saunter out to inspect the surface, rehearsing the Tony Greig pitch report. After you have tapped the pitch with your bat or hand, stepped on it with your cricket shoes to check the moisture content, and stared at the grass, the comments from every expert begin to flow: 'Oh, what a belter. I hope we win the toss and have a bat', 'Mate, is this a green top, or what!', 'This is sure to seam around early' or 'This one is sure to break up and spin out of the rough come day three or four'.

On this particular morning, the comments were

less than flattering. From all reports this same Trent Bridge pitch was used last week for the game between Nottingham and Yorkshire. As a result, glaring foot-holes at both ends and rough patches were mixed with thick grass patches. While Phil Tufnell and Paul Strang (Notts' Zimbabwean leg-spinner) were grinning like eager schoolkids, the other twenty players who were to be involved in the game were frowning like condemned murderers. Within moments, statements like 'You can't play on this, it hasn't been prepared' and 'You have to be bloody joking, this game will be over in two days' were dominating the centre-square discussion.

On initial inspection the pitch really was the ugliest I have seen. Although it was very hard under foot, the footholes were deep, and the grass, although not alarmingly green, was thick right down the centre and business end of the track. You could say it had everything a bowler would dream of: bare patches for the spinners, grass for the seamers and to top it all off, menacing, hanging clouds to assist the swingers. Keith Brown won the toss and batted, a very positive move in my view, even if the conditions may have suggested otherwise. An educated opinion would have predicted that this pitch could only deteriorate with time.

Fifteen minutes before lunch, all was going to plan and we were cruising at 97 for 0, but we went in to lunch at 97 for 3. We then lost our next seven wickets for 100 runs – an average effort as the world's ugliest pitch was playing like a flat Adelaide Oval batting paradise. In a nutshell we had a shocker, considering none of our wickets resulted from pitch assistance. The look really was deceiving, teaching me a very good lesson about judging a pitch purely by its appearance.

At stumps tonight the match is evenly balanced thanks largely to debutant Chris Batt, a tall, athletic, left-arm seamer who bowled aggressively, dismissing three of the Nottingham top-order batsmen. One of those batsmen was my old Australian Under-19 captain and team-mate Jason Gallian, who gave up life in Australia for an opportunity to play Test cricket for England. Now opening the batting for Nottingham and enjoying his life as a professional county cricketer in his adopted country, 'Gall' seems to have found his place in England. It seemed odd playing away from the Sydney Cricket Ground against the man who, in a funny sort of way, helped to kick-start my cricket career. As captain of the Australian Under-19s, ironically playing the England Under-19s, Gall cut his foot at Rottnest Island in Western Australia the day before the final youth Test at the WACA. His injury gave me an unexpected opportunity to play in the game. Luckily, I scored a few runs in the match which led to an invitation to the Australian Cricket Academy. From there, further great opportunities have presented themselves and, as they say, the rest is history. Fate is a funny thing!

Gall is now married to an English lass, he has played Test cricket for England and seems to be enjoying himself away from New South Wales where he learnt his cricket. Nottingham's gain may well be Australian, and certainly NSW, cricket's loss if the cover drives and cut shots he played today are anything to go by. Seeing the back of him was something of a relief as another session of his dominance could have put us out of the match, ugly pitch or no ugly pitch.

Thursday, 2 July – playing on a construction site

'Daa daa daa daa daa daa daa daa daa daa daa daa daa daa
Grr grr grr grr grr grr grr grr grr grr grr grr grr grr grr grr
Shh shh shh shh shh shh shh shh shh shh shh shh shh shh
Bang bang bang bang bang bang bang bang bang bang bang'

By stumps in Robin Hood's territory, everyone involved in the day's play had a pumping headache thanks to the sounds of yet another cricket ground construction site. If the number of these construction sites we have come across this summer is any indication, the future of English cricket grounds looks very sound. All England have to do now is start winning some Test matches and English cricket will be a most attractive commodity. Many of the counties seem to be developing their grounds into quite distinguished and illustrious stadiums to partner the already celebrated Lord's cricket arena.

When Mark Waugh took that catch at second slip to secure the Ashes last summer, the background at Trent Bridge was of open sky and a rickety old sightscreen. In twelve months this has all changed. Now the smart new grandstand, which houses corporate boxes, an indoor centre and ground-floor office space, provides the backdrop to the Nottinghamshire County Cricket Ground. This fresh construction adds immense character to a ground which until this year had quite a sleepy, uninviting aura about it.

Unfortunately, as with any new grand construction, the hubbub and commotion of a clattering drillpiece and drone of a frontend loader have a menacing effect on your brain after a few hours. It is hard enough concentrating on a cricket field without this added racket plaguing your thoughts. At six o'clock, the site whistle blew pervading the ground with heavenly silence; Gatt commented from first slip that, 'It's about bloody time!' After seven hours of banging and clanging and thumping and purring, the silence was most refreshing although the damage had been done as the nerves of every player and umpire had been tested to the last degree.

On the bright side, it will be worth putting up with a season or two of noise-works so that everyone can enjoy the fruits of the labours. The Lord's grandstand and its new media centre, and Nottingham's brand new colossus and indoor centre, are sure to add magnificence to England's cricket venues. It is a pity that this season we have to play cricket in surroundings more like a Beirut battlefield than a serene village cricket field, but in the end the headaches will all be worthwhile!

While the English stadiums will rival any in the world, the pain continued for Alec Stewart and his Test team today at Old Trafford. After losing the toss, the South Africans, recognised for their military-style discipline, were ruthless in their torture of the England bowling attack. At stumps they are 237 for 1. Jacques Kallis and Gary Kirsten were almost like heart surgeons clinically removing the heart of the England Test team with uncompromising precision. What they do with that heart remains to be seen, but if today is anything to go by they could be holding it and manipulating it as they please for the remainder of this Test match.

Friday, 3 July – English lunches

Mushy peas, toad-in-the-hole, spotted dick, Yorkshire pud and rosy lee – if I didn't know any better I would have mistaken this combination for the characters in a kid's cartoon series. But as I found out today, these are not Walt Disney inventions but part of our lunch menu at Trent Bridge. Rather than the standard 1.15 p.m. lunch break, I received a twenty-minute tutorial on the intricacies of English fine dining.

Mushy peas, a bright green slop, I am told are usually served best with your greasy fish'n'chips. Toad-in-the-hole is a mixture of sausages and a doughy batter served like a casserole, while spotted dick, as daunting as it sounds, is actually a sponge pudding filled with raisins and covered with custard or ice-cream. Yorkshire puds, of course, are a baked batter sort of thing served with your roast beef and loads of gravy. Bloody beautiful!

In this era of professionalism in sport, you would hardly describe this combination as your ideal athlete's lunch. It is not carbohydrates and re-hydrating sports drinks, but sometimes you just have to say 'What the heck?' sit back and indulge yourself with the tastes of northern England. Topped up with a few jam-filled biscuits and washed down with a warm cup of rosy lee you can't go wrong, if I say so myself.

Luckily, the lunch was good because that was about

the only treat we had for the day. England Under-19 vice-captain Paul Franks tore through our top order sending us crashing to a paltry score of only a few more runs than 100. My Middlesex team-mates and I had plenty of time to enjoy lunch as we lurched to an embarrassing defeat in two and a bit days. As predicted on day one, this game didn't go the distance, but I can confidently say that had nothing to do with the ugly cricket pitch, or the unathletic nutritional schedule.

Paul Franks is a young bowler with plenty of pace, aggression and attitude and I wouldn't be surprised to see him progress through the ranks. He bowls a good outswinger and he is aggressive in his approach to the game, admirable traits for a young aspirant. If he can remain fit and strong and continue to improve his bowling he has excellent potential. For the second game in a row I copped one in the helmet, thanks to this young fireball. If I am not careful I will finish my career shaking and slurring my words as a result of too many hits to the head!

In the Test match, the visitors continued their massacre on a very flat Old Trafford pitch. Gary Kirsten's double century was superb, while a Kallis century, Cullinan 75, and slow torture from Cronje and Rhodes simply added the gloss to what has been a dominant first two days for South Africa. England will have to fight for their lives in the remaining three days. The heart surgeons seem to be in control and having one hell of a time in Lancashire.

Saturday, 4 July – Donald is king!

How is it that Allan Donald can come out and make a flat Old Trafford pitch look like a lively Edgbaston one?

For two days we haven't seen a ball look the slightest bit menacing as the England fast bowlers toiled admirably for 200 overs, with little penetration or success. Kirsten, Kallis, Cullinan and Cronje made batting look as easy as riding a four-wheeler bike and yet Donald, on the same facility, had the English batsmen jumping around as though the lifeless turf had suddenly transformed into hot coals. Is it, as the majority of the English public seem to believe, that the English bowlers are simply no good?

If you ask me I don't think so! Darren Gough, Angus Fraser and Dominic Cork are all proven Test match bowlers who give more than a hundred per cent to their team's cause. I have never met a workhorse like Gus Fraser, and Darren Gough's charisma and ability to turn a game is well documented.

The difference, I believe, is that Allan Donald is simply in a higher class, one reserved for very few. Greatness is a word which should never be used lightly when describing the feats or talents of a sportsman, or anybody else for that matter. A player who has the ability consistently to change a game with his own hand, to make things happen when all seems lost, to lift the spirits of his team, and the game, through his own actions, is a great player. Warne, McGrath, Ambrose, Walsh, Wasim Akram and Waqar Younis are a few of the modern players who qualify for the title. Donald must also be on the list. Watching him bowl makes viewing cricket a pleasure, unless of course you are watching him from twenty-two yards away. Like watching Pete Sampras win Wimbledon, you know Donald is in total control as he breaks down his opponents.

Today, as he has done so many times in his career, it was he who lifted his team with a couple of spells of genuine, aggressive fast bowling. I asked Mark Ramprakash about him tonight on the phone and he said, 'The pitch is so flat, as you saw when we bowled. The only difference is that Donald just has that extra pace which seems to make batting that little bit harder.'

It is that undefined quality which makes Allan Donald the key player in this Test series. He really is the only truly great player, besides maybe Atherton and Stewart, in this series and unsurprisingly it could be he who holds the key to the outcome. Darren Gough may one day be a great bowler, as may Fraser or Cork, but until they consistently produce the goods like Donald, or, at times, Pollock, then England are always going to struggle on pitches like this Old Trafford one. I don't think England are that bad, I think Donald is just that good. Maybe my assessment of the English bowlers if I play them first-hand next Ashes series will differ from this, but at this stage I will stick to the 'Donald is king' view.

At stumps tonight England are eight wickets down and so many behind it will be hard for them to see the destination. With two days to go, the ball is definitely in the visitors', or at least in Allan Donald's, court.

Monday, 6 July – England fight back

So often the unsung hero with the ball, Angus Fraser was brilliant today in an alternative role. His effort at getting forward to Allan Donald, one of the world's fastest bowlers, was not only courageous, but also a vital part of England's fighting rearguard action to ensure that this Test series is still alive.

In a thrilling climax to the Test match, Gus saw out the final over, making heroes of himself and Robert Croft. South Africa must be pondering over what could, and possibly should, have been. After dominating the game, they looked certain to win, but even the great Allan Donald couldn't finish off the tail, which wagged like a happy dog.

Without claiming to be Nostradamus, England's fightback could turn out to be more significant than simply a saved match. The tourists would have used up a great deal of energy trying to win this Test, and they are going to have to work harder than ever to keep a rejuvenated England from going one step further in the fourth Test. Once again, time will tell.

Allan Donald returned inspiring figures of 6 for 88, but even that was not enough to give the South Africans a second Test victory which for four days looked certain to be theirs. Led by captain Alec Stewart, who batted like a man possessed, England should take a lot from their effort, although I imagine they will all be breathing a sigh of emotional relief after escaping looming Test defeat.

Stewart, Mike Atherton, Mark Ramprakash, Robert Croft and Gus Fraser all showed the grit and determination England need to be consistently competitive in

Test cricket. Although South Africa dominated much of this contest, England will know they are still in the battle. Had the South Africans won this, the real battle would have been over. With two Tests to go, England still have an opportunity to take an unlikely series victory. By following their captain's lead and by showing the same commitment as they have for the last five sessions of this Test, England will have the South Africans thinking closely about their tactics for the next Test.

For cricket's sake, after much discussion about the disappointing crowds during this Test, it is encouraging to have a live series still to play. More fighting performances and more victories by the home side will soon have the crowds back to Test cricket in England. Let's face it, no one likes to support a loser; you go to an event to feel good and enjoy a victory or at least a good fight. When England start offering this to the fickle public, I am sure the crowds will start to come back to the traditional game.

On a lighter note, Gus's heroics are sure to cause me aggravation over the next few days. For the last few months I have had to listen to his complaints about the hardships of being a fast bowler. We often argue, or at least discuss, whether the game is a contest that favours the bowlers or the batsmen. After today's effort, I am certain his argument will grow. Over the telephone tonight he continued his complaints.

'You know, I've got more publicity from facing thirteen balls with the bat than I have from taking one hundred and fifty Test wickets with the ball. That'd be bloody right, wouldn't it! You guys get all the praise, jeez it kills me.'

'Yeah, yeah Gus! Too bad you guys get all the opportunities in the world to make amends after bowling a pile of rubbish. We batsmen make one mistake and it's all over. No wonder we get all the praise. It's definitely a bowler's game.'

There is nothing like winding up a fast bowler. It doesn't matter whether I am on the field or off it, it is one of my favourite pastimes. This never-ending batsman versus bowler argument often takes over a post-match changing-room; it will never be settled. Every time the issue rears its comic head, each group seems to uncover yet another reason why they are the ones who have to work the hardest for their money. Even if the debate remains unresolved, we will have plenty of fun in the meantime agreeing to disagree.

Tuesday, 7 July – village cricket

English village cricket is a wonderful institution enjoyed by so many cricket-loving folk of all ages, sizes and backgrounds. Cricket played in the serenity of an English village ground offers something special to everyone involved.

It is heartening to see the managing director of an international sports company fielding at first slip alongside the local police constable and the local plumber. All three wait in anticipation for a ball being delivered by an eighteen-year-old, Jamaican-born youngster who works at the local garage and who has been given the day off because his boss is the chairman of the local club. This is not an unusual scene for a mid-week contest on the village green and it is also the beauty of village cricket. For a short period, everyone is equal in their pursuit of a brief moment of glory with bat or ball.

As a guest of the Faringham cricket club in Kent, I journeyed down the M25, over the Dartford toll bridge and into the sleepy but very pretty and colourful village of Faringham. Hidden away off the motorway, the picturesque but stamp-sized ground, dwarfed by green rolling hills on one side and thick forest on the other, made for a very tranquil setting for this friendly Tuesday afternoon fixture. Arriving just in time for afternoon tea, I sat with my hosts and drank cups of tea and picked at plates of sandwiches, chicken nuggets, cakes, biscuits and scones off the long chipboard tables.

'You would never get this sort of service at Lord's,' bragged one of the players, sipping his tea and tucking into his tenth mini sausage roll.

After the feast, and just like at Lord's, the bell rang to announce that the umpires would soon be on their way out to the middle. On hearing the chime, the players from the fielding side gulped the remainder of their tea, grabbed another handful of sandwiches and biscuits, made a few confident comments about having a look at their opening bowler, and with a wink, scampered down the steps and on to the ground. Having finished my tea, I sat down and observed the glorious spirit of village cricket. One of the opening batsmen, beer gut hanging over his trousers like a blown bubblegum hangs out of its chewer's mouth, struck a glorious pose as he prepared to walk to the crease with half a cheese and pickle sandwich sticking out of his mouth. As he scoffed the remains of his afternoon tea, he picked up his old sweat-destroyed gloves and the railway sleeper that he called his cricket bat, and walked out to the middle with his younger, skinnier partner.

His partner, a nervous-looking young chap, nodded at the senior player, and grinned apprehensively when he was told, with a serious expression, that he would be facing the first ball from that young garage worker from the next village. With no choice, and nowhere to hide, the younger opener took guard, nodded, winked and looked around the ground before preparing to face the first ball.

My host, who was actually the captain of the fielding team and supposed to be out commanding his team-mates, decided it would be rude not to sit and talk with me, so he sent his twelve-year-old son out to make up the required number.

As the young Jamaican 'quickie' marked out his long run-up, the bench skipper smiled at me and whispered, 'Have a look at this boy, he is *really* fast.'

All tall, black fast bowlers are, aren't they?

The stage was set. The old square-leg umpire, leaning on his walking stick, stood only ten metres from the rest of the batting order who were waiting to see the ferocity of the young paceman. As they watched, they sipped on their pints of warm beer, smoked their fags and joked about who would hit the most sixes. The hobbling umpire was so close to the crowd that he happily stood and continued his teatime conversation with his cigarette-smoking mate, who was amazingly standing behind the boundary rope.

Metric readings suggest that the Adelaide Oval and Lord's square boundaries are relatively short, but be assured, the Faringham cricket ground makes these boundaries look like Regent's Park. It was so short the cutters and pullers of this cricket world would have stood in the middle licking their lips at the prospect of tapping the ball for relatively easy fours and sixes. With nervous anticipation the boundary gallery watched as the opening bowler, obviously imitating Michael Holding, rhythmically flowed to the crease and let go of the first ball of the innings.

Fortunately there was no short-leg fieldsman in play on this fine summer's day, as he would have been in danger of losing his toes. The younger partner, ignoring the philosophy of blocking the first few balls in order to build an innings, stepped away towards square leg and swung his bat at the red-leather projectile as hard as his skinny, pale arms could muster. As I had suspected, the first ball was as erratic as the batsman's frame of mind, and rather than crashing into the stumps, the ball magnetically followed the batsman and thundered into his thigh.

In most cases it would have thundered into his thigh pad, but as we soon found out, he had forgotten to wear his thigh pad on this particular afternoon. As the batsman jumped around from square leg to point and back again, the crowd roared with laughter at the obvious discomfort being shown. Shouts of 'Keep your eye on the ball' and 'Get on with it, you bloody wimp' echoed from the pavilion steps. The poor fellow, who probably hadn't picked up a bat for weeks, and who had probably never faced anything as quick as the Jamaican garage worker, eventually smiled at his mates, waved his hand, and faced up for his next delivery.

After bruise one, the game progressed and the West

Indian fast bowler, whose run-up and complexion gave him a distinct and automatic psychological advantage, finished his first spell with 0 for 42 off six overs. It wasn't so much that he had bowled poorly, it was more a case that the short square boundaries and slow pitch caused him more frustration than a rusted bolt at work.

With little technique, all of the visiting batsmen swung at the ball as hard as they may at a golfball with a one wood. In a single afternoon I have never seen so many mis-hit sixes over the point and third man regions. Balls were flying everywhere, much to the disgust of the opposition bowlers, who could have mistaken their afternoon cricket game for a visit to the driving range at St Andrews.

As for us spectators, we all took great humour and delight from the proceedings. Just being there, watching a friendly game of cricket and enjoying the atmosphere, was a marvellous escape from the rigours of the county circuit. Seeing the joy and satisfaction being gained by all the participants, including the kids running around on the grass, helped highlight even further the wonderful soul of this wonderful game.

It is all quite different in Australia where the system of cricket is much more structured than in England. We have a distinct path from junior cricket and school cricket through to club cricket, state cricket and ultimately international cricket. This allows for an effective talent identification process; not many of the talented young fish escape the net. Remember how I mentioned that on my debut in grade cricket, I was playing in the same match as Messrs Lillee, Alderman and Hughes – how many English club cricketers have that sort of introduction?

Obviously, the thousands of people who have no real desire to play cricket for any other reason than having fun can play in various organised competitions. It is rare to drive around Perth on the weekend and see a cricket field not in use. Games vary from the ultra competitive to the beer-bellied lads having the time of their lives.

The form of cricket that we can boast proudly about is beach cricket. Beach cricket is similar to English village cricket in many regards. We play it in idyllic settings with long white sandy beaches acting as the playing field. Anyone and everyone joins in the fun under the heavenly blue skies, in and out of the royal blue ocean and playing with a smile and a laugh at all times.

There is nothing like playing beach cricket on a warm summer's day just as the sun is setting. In Australia we probably take the sensational sunsets for granted because we see them so often, but when you are down on the beach just before it disappears into the ocean, you know that you are living. Like a pint of beer in the bar of a village cricket ground, a beer and fish'n'chips, or a picnic, after a game of beach cricket is a marvellous experience.

By stumps, the visitors had managed to hold out for a closely fought draw. Plenty of beer had been drunk, there had been a few heroes on the park, but most importantly everyone had had a fantastic day out. As I left the small but warm clubhouse, with the sun slowly starting to disappear, I could see that the most heroic feats were just about to begin in the bar. After a few more well-earned pints, I am sure those sixes will have turned into the 'biggest six I have ever seen' and the Jamaican speedster will have gained a reputation as 'the fastest bowler in the world'. I think I left just in time! Here's to village cricket. Cheers.

CHAPTER TEN

Testing Times

Wednesday, 8 July – English umpires

Umpire David Shepherd has become legendary over the years for his 'hop, skip and jump' on Nelson while officiating at all levels of the game. Like Richie Benaud's commentary, Don Bradman's cover drive or the fight for the Ashes, David's little antics will always be remembered and enjoyed in all cricket circles. They have become so much a part of the game that he is often seen in the cricket highlights performing his entertaining 'jig of superstition'.

Fielding at square leg today I grinned in admiration as the Durham scorecard ticked over to 111 for 1. To continue the legendary tradition, 'Shep' started his hopping from one leg to another, until the score had eventually been substituted for another less superstitious total. Not one to let an opportunity pass, I asked 'Shep' about his dancing prowess on the cricket field. In his normal polite way he simply smiled and spent the next three overs at square leg defining the English 'Nelson' theory. He then explained how it would be impossible to forget about his gestures, because on the odd occasion that he does forget to peek at the scoreboard, the crowd is now very quick to remind him.

'The crowd love it,' he said. 'I do it for them now, and if they enjoy it, then that is good enough for me,' he finished with a smile.

Chatting with one of England's most respected Test umpires, it made me realise how good the standard of umpiring is in this country. One thing we in Australia can learn from English county cricket focuses on this point. The English circuit has many excellent umpires who could easily take the step up to the international panel. One of the reasons the English umpires are so good is that the majority have played the game before, giving them the advantage of being able to read the game and interpret and react to any situations which may arise. Having the experience of cricket in their blood allows them to be very aware of the game and its laws.

Not only do they understand the game, but there are also a number of great characters among them whom you could easily have a beer with after a day's play and enjoy a good cricket conversation with. While they all have their own characteristics, the list is long of the good English umpires. For example, Peter Willey, who looks as tough as Clint Eastwood behind the stumps and 'calls a spade a spade', is one of the good ones going around.

Roy Palmer, the Rupert Murdoch-style entrepreneur, has more ideas than the media magnate himself and is no doubt a better cricket umpire to go along with it. Then there is Smiling Ray Julian, who is said to have the fastest hand in the West, and always provides plenty of entertainment to the cricket field. Kenny Palmer makes it quite obvious when a player should be on his way with a loud 'that's out' or 'that's not out', whatever he sees fit. Dickie Bird needs no introduction from me, except that he is a true cricket icon all over the world, and Merv Kitchen, the old Somerset boy, is a top bloke and bloody good umpire.

Graham 'Budgie' Burgess has been something of a good luck charm for me this summer. He has umpired in four of the games that I have been lucky enough to have scored centuries, so I will be asking him at the end of the summer to volunteer for any games that I will be playing in, in the future.

In 1995 I unfortunately had a run-in with umpire Alan Whitehead while captaining a Young Australian eleven at Cardiff. He threatened to send off our young fast bowler for bowling a beamer at one of the Glamorgan batsmen. After heated discussion, Mark Harritty was allowed to continue his bowling spell but I don't think Alan took too kindly to the young Australian's attitude towards the game. Remembering the incident, I spoke to Alan before my first game of the season as a county cricket player. After a brief rekindling of this incident, we were able to have a laugh that day at Old Trafford, and we seem to have got along very well since. As a stickler for the rules and etiquette of the game I have a lot of respect for his rulings on the game.

If you ever need to relax and enjoy a good chat on the field, you can't go past John Holder; while John Hampshire umpires a lot like an Australian plays his cricket. John is also one of the outstanding 'umps' on the circuit. Vanburn Holder, Nigel Plews, Chris Balderstone, David Constant, Allan Jones, Trevor Jesty, Barry Leadbeater, George Sharp, 'Jerry' Lloyds, the list goes on. During the whole season I can't think of one incident with any of these umpires that would cause a stir. English cricket certainly has it right by employing this quality of umpires who help the county circuit run smoothly and efficiently. My hat goes off to English umpires who truly set the standard for umpiring in world cricket.

Thursday, 16 July – the time difference

The time difference is always a problem when your other life is on the far side of the world. Between my home town in Perth, Western Australia, and West Hampstead in London we are talking about a seven-hour difference; London to Melbourne, the business capital of Australia, has a nine-hour variance. This law of nature isn't usually anything more than an accepted part of living away from home, but at times it escalates into unbearable frustration especially when you have an important phone call to make back to Australia.

After receiving a message on my mobile-phone message bank this afternoon, my mind was sent into a frenzy. Australian Cricket Board chief executive Malcolm Speed was the reason for my speeding brainwaves. I couldn't help but wonder exactly why the ACB boss needed to speak to me so urgently.

With nine hours' difference between London and Melbourne, I found myself with an awkward dilemma. Obviously the word 'urgent' at the close of his message had me scratching my head and weighing up my two options for contacting the ACB office, particularly the office of the chief. Do I wait until midnight and reach the boss as soon as he walks into the office in Melbourne? Or do I control my curious mind and wait patiently for a phone call in the morning?

Patience is not one of my strong points and curiosity would normally have got the better of me, but a long day in the field was taking its toll and I begrudgingly went to bed at around 10.00 p.m. My attempt at sleep was fruitless. Mind games took over as every possible conversation with my Australian employer and chief of Aussie cricket ran through my brain like a rampant steam train. Between 11.30 and midnight, three calls to the Melbourne office turned out to be as futile as my attempts to sleep. An answering machine was my only response, a frustration at the best of times. Tired of swearing at a recorded voice message and sick of ignoring my tired eyes, I decided to try to sleep through the anxiety.

My bedside clock told me that it was 7.00 a.m. when the phone rang. The boss beat me to it and saved me from the nervous tension of tapping in the long-distance numbers on my telephone. Fortunately, all the worrying thoughts that had plagued me turned out to be unnecessary. The reason for the call was the one I least expected. Down the phone line from Melbourne, I heard Malcolm's voice warmly saying, 'Congratulations Justin, you have been selected in the touring party for Pakistan. Well done, you deserve the selection, and I am thrilled to be able to give you this good news personally.' What a way to be woken up in the morning!

An unbelievable feeling of joy, pride and some relief pumped through my veins. It wasn't until I had put down the phone that the realisation started to dawn upon me. I am part of the Australian cricket team again. Words are too shallow to describe the feeling. Reselection for the Australian cricket team is an incredible moment. Unfortunately, it was ruined, or at least diluted, by the fact that I was by myself in a hotel room in the middle of nowhere with no wife and child, and no one to hug and jump up and down with on the bed; that was a disappointment. It was also too early to crack open a magnum of champagne and enjoy the material taste of success.

By the end of this summer, I could have benefited more from a season of county cricket than I may ever have imagined. Not only will I have played a lot of cricket in varying conditions and improved my game, but by the look of this morning's proceedings, my early season success for Middlesex could have helped sway the selectors when they picked the touring squad. Who knows whether it helped my cause, I guess only the selectors know that, but in the end my runs in these foreign conditions could only have helped. In September, I think I will be leaving England for Pakistan owing county cricket a huge hand of gratitude, greater than I may ever have thought.

Monday, 20 July – cricket in the dark

I was warned! Yet after all the warnings and advice, I could never have prepared for today's unusual affair as a county cricketer.

The warnings and advice were along the lines of, 'If cricket day in, day out doesn't get you, the travel up and down the motorway is sure to drive you mad.'

Overseas players from different countries and cultures have generally reflected this attitude when talking of the grind of the county circuit. Even the most experienced and seasoned of English county pros had warned me from day one that a county season would be like nothing I had experienced before in my short cricket career. Lying in bed tonight, I thought that all the words in the *Oxford Dictionary* couldn't have prepared me for this week's fiasco.

Having just played four days of championship cricket, the legs and brain were already showing signs of fatigue and distraction; nothing to worry about, but enough to have the calf muscles and brainwaves starting to ask a few questions. Sure, there is nothing unusual about four days' cricket; that is what we get paid for and, for that matter, we are very accustomed to playing four days straight. The twist in this ridiculous caper doesn't even set in after playing a Sunday League game yesterday. Five days in a row is no big deal; it's just like playing a Test match that goes the full distance. County players are accustomed to contesting a forty-over game the day after, or in between, a championship match, making five days of play. No complaints, everyone is used to that, even though you are generally physically and mentally drained after five days on the park.

The complaint today is that after finishing yesterday's 'pseudo' Test match, we had to pack up our five-day changing-room at Guildford and travel directly to Hove in Sussex to make our preparations for tonight's day/night fixture against Sussex. As it would be pointless showering and making ourselves beautiful for a training session in two hours' time, we all decided to put up with each other's body odour and bad breath and hit the motorway as quickly as possible. After packing the cars to the brink of bursting, we left the lovely Guildford cricket ground in our coloured cricket clothes and made the journey to yet another new cricket destination.

A stop at the local petrol station allowed the boys to fill up with chocolate bars, ice-cream, crisps and soft drinks – a perfect athlete's diet again to get ready for the following day's play. Exactly the preparation that any professional sportsman needs to perform at their optimum, I don't think.

It gets better! The Middlesex first eleven arrived at the Sussex County Cricket Ground at 9.00 p.m. in excellent spirits. After an hour and a half's car journey, which included a nutritious pre-training meal of rubbish, a final-ball defeat in the Sunday League game, and let's not forget a flogging in the championship game for the four previous days, everyone was feeling on top of the world.

The plan for last night was to spend an hour practising under the portable Sussex lights to give the players an opportunity to adjust to the conditions which are foreign to all of my team-mates. Being the consummate professional, coach John Buchanan thought it essential that the guys spend some time taking a few catches and adjusting to the game under lights. Although everyone was a little jaded and flat, there was a sense of excited and curious anticipation as we walked on to the ground to test the new lights.

Unfortunately, the training session didn't go exactly to plan. Before the session kicked off, we had a team meeting in the centre of the ground. After a few indifferent performances, we collectively decided to use the meeting as a team honesty session. There is no substitute for honesty with yourself and your team-mates and the only way to seek real answers is to ask the tough questions. In other words, we were all intent on getting to the heart of the issues that were concerning and affecting the Middlesex team performances. At times, the honesty became light-heartedly heated as we endeavoured to find solutions to our petering performances.

Like a political debate, every member of the team was allowed to say their piece and put across their point of view on what parts of our game could be improved. By eleven o'clock the discussion was raging hot and real progress was being made; answers were being found to the questions that were on every player's mind. Then the Sussex authorities decided enough was enough.

In their wisdom and, more appropriately, their wish to go home from work, the authorities obviously figured there was only one solution. For them, the best way to extinguish our enthusiastic preparation for the day/night encounter, and for that matter the remainder of our season, was to turn off the lights and leave us out in the cold and, literally, in the dark. Here we were, solving the problems of the world, and all of a sudden we were left deserted in the centre of a dew-drenched county cricket ground wondering how to find our way back to the pavilion.

It would have been easy to make our way back to the warmth and light of the changing-room, and particularly the hot showers, but instead our discussion continued like an Oprah Winfrey talk show. The only problem now was that our team talk was taking place in a very misty darkness. So dark was it that I didn't see, but I have my suspicions, which one of my team-mates walked up behind me and gave me a couple of kidney punches in protest at what was supposed to be constructive criticism.

One of the boys had obviously taken offence at my straight-talking comments on improving our fitness, or playing with a little more passion, and decided the best way to answer my suggestions was with a touch of physical retaliation. Luckily for my tormentor, the ground was so dark that you couldn't see within a couple of inches of your own nose so I am not a hundred per cent sure of who was battering my kidneys as if he was trying to tenderise a piece of rump steak. It was fortunate I was unable to catch the culprit because I've got a feeling that 'Rock'n'Wrestling No. 25,000' may have broken loose in the middle of the cricket ground if I had got my hands on my Mike Tyson team-mate. After heated discussion, five days' cricket, time on the road and sore feet, no one, including me, was in any mood to take a backward step from this 'Oprah' scenario.

Bruised ribs and dented egos aside, I must admit it was a relief having the opportunity to enjoy an hour of open discussion with my team-mates who are all as keen for success as I am. The county season is so long that the opportunity for close inspection of your own game and the team performance can become restricted. Even though we were left in the dark, the discussion within the team was helpful therapy for everyone. In the short term, our discussion may have proved fruitless as we played poorly in tonight's encounter, but in the bigger picture I believe it could have a positive effect on building a much stronger foundation.

Six days straight is a marathon in cricket terms and considering we start a championship game against

Yorkshire on Wednesday, the ultra marathon is about to get started. By eight o'clock next Sunday night, I will have completed eleven days of cricket out of twelve. That's one hell of a lot of cricket in any person's language! It seems insane that after a match a team has no chance to analyse the game and learn from it, as they are off to another venue for a late-night training session and a game the next day.

Maybe this really is one of the big problems with English cricket?

Never before have I played a day's cricket and travelled fifty miles on a motorway for more cricket. No one loves the game more than I do, but by the time we had eventually checked into our new hotel at midnight last night you may never have known this. My frame of mind was pushing more towards the negative than the positive about life as a professional cricket player. Luckily, today's game didn't start until 5.00 p.m. so I had at least a little time to recharge the batteries.

The general consensus about English cricket, as I have touched upon many times this summer, suggests that English county players are playing far too much. This is a problem that may act as the catalyst to weaken the standard and intensity of the county game, in turn impacting upon the inconsistent performances of the Test team. There is no more glaring example than this last six days straight.

It seems absurd that Angus Fraser, just selected for the fourth Test against South Africa commencing on Thursday, today played his sixth day straight. He will be expected to be at his best for his country come Thursday, yet his fast bowler's body and mind have only two days to recover from a tiring and potentially destructive campaign of county cricket. The question being asked is 'How are players expected to be consistently fresh and at their best when the county programme demands such massive outputs of physical and mental energy from its players?'

Cricket, cricket, cricket – great for the lovers of the game, spectating from the grandstands or in front of their television sets, but daunting for the players, no matter how great their love affair with the game. Something has to suffer and if history is any indication perhaps it is English cricket as a whole.

Friday, 24 July – perseverance and reverse sweeps

Three days are a long time in this fickle game of cricket. Only two days ago Angus Fraser was a little pensive, even philosophical, about his chances of being selected for the fourth Test at Trent Bridge. Being selected for the squad of thirteen was a relief, and it wasn't until yesterday morning that he knew that he was in the final eleven. The critics have been writing him off saying that he is past his best and lacks the penetration of his earlier years. As he has done so many times before, he answered those critics as only he knows how. With the cricket ball as his only weapon, he took to his task like a bird takes to building her nest. One ball at a time, pushing in like an old steam train, he earned his just reward on the stage he so cherishes, with another magnificent five-wicket haul against the South Africans. No other player epitomises the work ethic as does my Middlesex team-mate. He stands out on the county circuit as one of the few players who is totally dedicated to playing for his country no matter what it takes. His effort in this first innings is truly a most deserved reward.

At stumps, England are fighting hard to even up the series. Mark Butcher repaid the selectors' faith with a fine opening stand with Mike Atherton, but once again it was that man Allan Donald who broke the partnership and changed the course of the afternoon. The game hangs in the balance on this, day two, with the question being asked, 'Will the revamped middle order be able to show the same character as their workhorse fast bowler Gus Fraser?'

At Lord's today I started to understand why Mike Gatting played that infamous reverse sweep in the World Cup final against Australia. So often mocked for that one false shot, Gatt showed me today why he would have backed himself to play the reverse sweep, even under pressure.

Setting up a run chase for Yorkshire tomorrow, Gatt had the opportunity to reverse sweep the spinners this afternoon. Over and over again he played the shot with the same ease as Allan Donald bowls an outswinger. He hit it with such precision and power that on at least four occasions the fieldsmen didn't even bother to chase the ball to the boundary.

One of the facets of English cricket that I have admired since playing county cricket is the batsmen's ability to improvise. As a result of opportunities in the middle, a great number of the English batsmen seem to be able to play a great array of strokes to all degrees of a cricket field. Particularly in the one-day game, batting improvisation expands scoring opportunities and makes it difficult for the opposition to contain a fast scoring rate.

If I could play the reverse sweep with the ease and control of the former England captain, I think I would also play it with the same regularity. Whether I'd do it in a World Cup final is another question but it doesn't surprise me now that he tried it. I am sure that continued exposure to this style of batting from the great players like Gatt will prove beneficial to my game.

Sad news today as I learnt that a little buddy of mine from Western Australia has just lost his epic battle with leukaemia. One of the worst aspects of living and working away from home for an extended period is receiving news like we received today. One of life's greatest fighters, Kyle will be sadly missed. His battle against the cruellest of diseases is now over. Although it beat him in the end he fought a fight which would have made Ali, Churchill and William Wallace proud. My heart goes out to his mum, dad and family whose loss can never be described in words.

It puts it all in perspective, doesn't it?

Saturday, 25 July – Boof and Tuffers

Look up the entry for Friday, 22 May about dropped catches. About halfway through you will see the words, 'A let-off or reprieve from the opposition must work as a kind of alarm bell to wake the player up for the day ahead. Rarely do you see a top-line player given a chance without making the opposition pay for the mistake. The old adage about catches winning matches, oh how true it is!' Unfortunately, it was me who dropped my Australian mate Darren 'Boof' Lehmann on the first ball he faced today at Lord's. As the ball slipped through my fingers, I cringed at the thought of the alarm bell ringing in Boof's mind, which was sure to click him into his concentration zone. What may have been a quiet ringing in his mind sounded like a screaming, banging, brass band in mine.

Sure enough, my theory wasn't disproved as Boof's second ball was smashed back past the bowler for four, pushing this classy overseas pro into second gear, ready to flick into third and fourth for the remainder of the afternoon. He was away and I was dreading the result.

Remarkably, he didn't reach triple figures but his 93 was enough to save Yorkshire from an outright defeat. At one stage he was so dominant it looked as though his adopted county might pull off an unlikely victory. Fortunately for Middlesex, he fell short of his century and my misjudgement at second slip wasn't as costly as it was threatening to be for much of the sunny afternoon.

Although the game ended in a draw, Boof demonstrated his rare ability to the appreciative crowd. Watching his battle against Phil Tufnell was intriguing. Tuffers was bowling into a patch of rough that resembled a family-pizza-sized dust pit, yet still Boof continued to sweep and cut England's best spinner (in my opinion). A battle like this, between two outstanding first-class cricketers, is especially pleasing to the cricket purist; such a confrontation may be viewed in the same way as a duel between two chess masters. The problem with county cricket is that you don't see enough duels like this. First-class cricket should involve top-class players fighting battles of mind and body on the field, and this battle between two top-class left-handers was a purist's dream.

It is great to see Tuffers regaining his confidence and bowling with the same aggression and control as the Aussies experienced at The Oval last summer. He is a fine bowler who, in my view, is a class above other spinners in this country. By believing a little more in his own ability, and realising that he is a genuine match winner, Tuffers could play many more Test matches for England. Although he didn't dismiss Boof today, he took giant steps towards getting back to his best.

After the game, members of both teams ventured into the famous Lord's Tavern. Listening to Tuffers and Boof talking about the day's proceedings prolonged the intrigue of the battle. Both guys discussed the duel and suggested different methods of attack for next time. 'You should have come around the wicket,' suggested Boof, who was advised by the wily spinner that he was lucky not to get out, sweeping out of the rough. As the discussion deepened, it was interesting to hear how each player was trying to get the upper hand over the other. You usually find that the top players talk a lot about the game with each other. Great Australian Test captain Ian Chappell preaches the importance of talking about the game among each other and with your peers. The culture of Sheffield Shield cricket in Australia promotes open discussion at the end of every day's play. 'It is where you learn so much about the game,' I have heard Ian say so many times. 'Listening to the best players talking about cricket is the best forum for learning about the game,' he has told me over and over.

County cricket doesn't seem to promote this culture as enthusiastically. This is more a result of players leaving the changing-rooms very soon after the end of a day's play rather than lack of interest. With the county players playing so much cricket, it is generally accepted that a player leaves the ground to return to the motorway or his family within twenty minutes of stumps. It is a pity because the opportunity for precious learning, especially for the younger players, is being wasted. If you are not there, it is impossible to learn anything.

Tonight being an exception to the norm, the discussion was healthy and improving with every pint of lager. As far as I am concerned, as a player eager to accelerate my learning curve, there is only one thing better than 'talking good cricket' and that is 'playing good cricket'. Whether watching it from first slip like today or with the bat in my hand, the game is an open classroom.

Today was an enjoyable learning experience both on and off the magical Lord's field. Perhaps the next time Boof and Tuffers meet will be at the Sydney Cricket Ground in a few months' time during the Ashes battle. I look forward to watching the rematch of the 'lefties', even if I won't be watching from first slip when these two continue their fight in Australia. I can also confidently predict that next time I will not be as keen to see the back of Boof as I was today.

Monday, 27 July – one-all and England are fighting back

My humble prediction two months ago when the Test

series, an important one for England, kicked off against the South Africans was that England would have to match South Africa for discipline, desire and determination to have a chance of winning it. The last five days have helped revitalise this theory as England fought like wounded dogs to revive the soul of their proud game. For five days of this enthralling Trent Bridge Test match, the home team have shown the fight, discipline and determination necessary to compete with and ultimately defeat their opponents. By achieving these key components, they have consequently earned the reward of an equalising Test match victory.

We witnessed and enjoyed some magnificent and encouraging individual performances. Angus Fraser fought like a heavyweight boxer. He threw punches, took punches and eventually knocked out his opponent in the twelfth round. On receiving his man-of-the-match award, he must really have felt like a pummelled heavyweight boxer, exhausted, but proudly hanging the champion's belt over his bruised and swollen shoulder as he left the ring.

From Mike Atherton, we witnessed an innings of outstanding concentration, skill and courage that must inspire not only his team-mates but all those young dreamers out there who aspire to play Test cricket. He stood up to one of a batsman's greatest enemies, Allan Donald, and fought for six hours before emerging victorious. It was a magnificent, yet characteristic, leader's knock.

In the first innings, Mark Ramprakash batted as if not only his livelihood but also his life depended upon the way he played his next ball. The look in his eye was so fiercely determined that he would have made his daughter nervous had she seen the change in her daddy.

At the end of it all, Alec Stewart walked to the crease and batted like a dragon slayer determined to kill off the monster and lead his troops, as victors, into the final battle. He batted with such aggression and control that he treated the South African bowlers with an arrogance that can lift his team to a higher level of achievement and expectation.

Richie Benaud commented as the victory celebrations returned to the England changing-room, that England's victory meant a lot for English cricket, not only in keeping this series alive but also in enhancing the team's prospects for the upcoming Ashes series in Australia. If the England team can reverse the trends of the last decade and continue to play this same brand of fighting cricket, their fortunes must look brighter.

As I left Lord's today, one of the old attendants laughed and said to me, 'I hope they don't get too carried away JL, one good match doesn't make a summer, does it?' Ever the optimists, these English cricket supporters. No wonder playing for England must at times feel like a life sentence.

Well done England on a meritorious Test match victory.

CHAPTER ELEVEN

Still Searching for the Currant Bun

Tuesday, 28 July – cricket robots!

Here he goes again, you are probably thinking when I reiterate that popular opinion in this country suggests that there is too much cricket played by English players. Too much cricket potentially leads to a situation where every day is just another day at the office for many of the players who earn their living from wearing cream flannels and shining a red leather ball around their groin region. A complacent attitude is a dangerous attitude for any player aspiring to break out of county cricket and step up into the fire of the Test match arena. The jump is a large one, but one that should be treasured and fought for with unrivalled determination and discipline.

Yesterday England won a Test match, an outstanding victory worth celebrating, not only because of the win itself but also because they now find themselves in a position of strength. They can take a Test series against one of the game's power teams. Let's face it, it is not every day that you win a Test match, and for England it is not as if it has been happening very often. Considering the current focus on the state of English cricket, it would have been appropriate for the English players to savour yesterday's monumental victory and enjoy the high emotions of a Test match success. You, or at least I, thought that the England players would have had the party of a lifetime last night, enjoyed the moment and enjoyed every emotion for as long as they possibly could, or at least for as long as their wives or partners would allow.

Instead, my spies tell me that half an hour after the game the home changing-rooms at Trent Bridge were half empty with most of the team back on the motorway returning home for a NatWest quarter-final today. So was yesterday just another day at the office for a lot of these guys?

Steve Waugh said to me last summer, 'Mate, that's one of the big problems with English cricket. What is the point of playing a game if you don't celebrate and enjoy a victory?'

To me, a big part of playing Test cricket for Australia is the aftermath of a victory and the changing-room scene which follows. After working hard under pressure for five days, there is no greater feeling than walking back into the changing-room and listening to the team songs 'Khe San' and 'True Blue' before the climax of the celebration begins. Standing arm in arm with your sweaty mate, five days' growth on your face, beer in hand, David Boon, or more recently Ian Healy, stands on a table and sings the team chorus of 'Underneath the Southern Cross we stand . . .'. To say this is uplifting and inspiring is an understatement. The feeling is euphoric and motivating. It is like an addictive drug: the more you get the more you want. It makes playing and winning for Australia a very special experience.

It is from this experience that my confusion about an empty England dressing-room stems.

Standing in the slips today at Lord's, I posed the question to Mike Gatting – England selector, former England captain and, of course, an English batting supremo and party lover. Who better to ask than a man who has lived and breathed English cricket for the last two and a half decades? I started the conversation with a statement.

'Gatt, Gus has just played five days of Test cricket. Less than twenty-four hours ago he was on the winning side in a Test match and won the man-of-the-match award. It seems crazy that he is opening the bowling for Middlesex at ten this morning! That's a fairly tough ask, not only on his body, but also considering that the emotions must still be running high from yesterday. How could he possibly truly enjoy an event like yesterday when he knew that the next morning he would be doing it all again? Same job, just a different team, a different venue, a different atmosphere. I know Gus and Ramps cherish playing for Middlesex and they would never question playing today, but surely the fact that there is a game scheduled for the day after a Test match is a problem with the system?'

Playing a Test match is an exhausting experience, where the pressures and stresses leave you just plain worn out. When you put your heart and soul into one event for five days, you need to have some sort of break to recuperate your energies and enjoy the memory of the experience.

Over the course of the day our discussion continued and I came to the conclusion that everyone in England probably agrees that it is a constantly tough ask, particularly on the Test players, but unfortunately the ultimate conclusion is, 'That's just the way it is over here, mate.'

It seems ironic that over this English summer I have written about this subject on many occasions. Too much cricket? It sounds like it, doesn't it. For me, playing cricket every day is like heaven on earth. I am loving it, but I honestly believe it would be different if I was playing the same amount of cricket in Australia and still aspiring to play for my country. Even my spirit for the game is starting to wane as the months of county cricket tick by, and I haven't got anywhere near the commitments of the England players while I am in this country.

Unfortunately, I can see that some things are bound to suffer as a result of this conveyor-belt system of cricket day in, day out. Perhaps it will be the standard of play, the intensity of the attitudes, the longevity of the players, the interest of the public, or the desire and determination of the players. Perhaps it will simply be that cricket is no longer seen as a game to be enjoyed and cherished but rather as a job where nothing else matters except turning up so that you can pay the bills. That would be sad.

In the *Collins Gem Dictionary*, game is defined as 'a contest for amusement; pastime; jest'. If people lose sight of the fact that cricket is a game, a great game, I believe we are losing the point of it.

Today simply reinforced this to me. It is a shame, in my opinion, that the England players can't enjoy the game to its fullest. Such a congested programme takes away some of the glitter and reason for playing.

Even the most élite of performers need time to enjoy their successes, blow off steam and let their hair down occasionally. If players cannot do this, they will turn into robots who are living off quick-fix adrenalin and money. Who wants to watch performing robots, and for that matter who wants to be a performing robot? I bet if they had the choice, guys like Angus Fraser and Mark Ramprakash, yesterday's heroes, would love time to enjoy a job well done. They obviously can't come out and say it, but even though it was nice to have them both playing for Middlesex today, in the bigger picture, it was sad to see them out on the park after what they went through yesterday.

Wednesday, 29 July – John Buchanan

It just didn't feel right! On Monday afternoon I made my way down to Lord's to show an old mate of mine the home changing-rooms and give him a personal tour of the ground. As we were sitting on my favourite balcony and chatting about old times, I couldn't help but notice the enthusiasm of the Hampshire team as they made their way onto the ground for a pre-NatWest quarter-final training session. As with so many opposition teams visiting Lord's, the energy and exuberance shines out like a lighthouse on the White Cliffs of Dover.

The feeling that didn't seem right was that Hampshire were fine-tuning their skills the day before the important quarter-final while we were having a day off. Now as history will tell you, Hampshire thrashed us yesterday in the quarter-final, and although missing a training session the day before wasn't the sole reason, it couldn't have helped.

Frustrated by the decision not to prepare the day before for the important game, coach John Buchanan dropped a bit of a bombshell last night. To the shock of all at the club, and a few of the players, the headlines in the paper this morning read: 'TURMOIL AT MIDDLESEX' and 'THE DECLINE OF MIDDLESEX'. Even though the headlines were a little exaggerated the article suggested that Buck was disappointed with the way we had prepared for the game, and that he didn't feel that he had the full support of a couple of his senior players. Now in a club with the tradition and standing of the Middlesex County Cricket Club this was not going to go down too well. To say that there were a few raised eyebrows is something of an understatement.

It has been an interesting summer for Middlesex's new Australian coach. Maybe he should be writing this book instead of me?

When I heard that John had been employed by Middlesex to take over the coaching position I was very excited to say the least. Having seen his outstanding success with the Queensland cricket team in Australia, I was delighted that I was going to work with this coaching dynamo first hand. Playing against him at home, we are always marvelling at 'the coach with the clipboard and laptop computer' and wondering what the hell he does with all his writing and typing. Knowing that we would now be working together I figured that all these questions would be answered as this summer unfolded.

I was thrilled at this prospect of seeing cricket analysis at a new level.

The way John has visibly transformed the Queensland cricket set-up has been a credit to his skills as a person, a coach and a manager. It would be fair to say that Queensland cricket has been at the forefront in the introduction of true professionalism since he took over at the helm five years ago. You only have to talk to his players to understand what an impact he has made on their cricket. They all speak so highly of him that he must have a lot to offer on, and off, the cricket field.

When you play against Queensland you always feel as though they have done their homework when you walk out into the middle. Having built up an extensive library of video and technical data on all of the players around Australia, the Queenslanders are never short of ample playing information to plot a cricket assassination for any of their opposition players, Any game against the Queensland Bulls is always going to be a 'scrap' until the final siren as a result of their thorough preparation.

When the Middlesex hierarchy decided to employ Buck it was obviously these high credentials that looked so attractive. He had done it for Queensland cricket, who had never won a Sheffield Shield until he took over, so the hope was that he would also help to transform the flagging fortunes of Middlesex cricket. It would be fair to say though, and I am sure that Buck would be the first to admit it, that at this stage he hasn't had the same fundamental success with this county side that he has had with his Australian Sheffield Shield side.

The reasons for this are varied, but fundamentally I believe it has come down to a difference in philosophy and method between the coach and a couple of the senior members of the Middlesex County Cricket Club. Like any change, Buck's style of coaching was always going to take some getting used to. A stickler for thoroughness of preparation, it has been a little frustrating watching Buck fight the hectic system of county cricket.

Having played county cricket for so many collective years, I can see how Gatt, Keith Brown and newly appointed skipper Mark Ramprakash have found it more difficult to adapt to this new style of coaching. In the early days of his reign as Queensland coach Buck had to sell his style to senior players Allan Border, Craig McDermott and Carl Rackemann and, after initial teething problems, he earned their respect and ultimately a Sheffield Shield victory. Unfortunately the initial teething problems don't seem to have been solved at this stage of the season, hence the article in tonight's *Evening Standard* newspaper. It seems to me that there has been an initial communication problem that has led to more communication breakdowns between the coach, the captain and a few other senior players.

Traditionally the captains of Middlesex, namely Mike Brearley and Mike Gatting, who between them held the position from 1971 to 1997, have pretty much run the show. From selection to training to preparation the captain has been the sole general, with the assistance of coach Don Bennett. When Ramps took over the job as Middlesex captain, I get the impression that he was asked to continue this strong traditional role of captain.

The breakdown seems to have come in the fact that John Buchanan, who is used to running the show in Queensland, was also told that he should take control. It seems to me that he was assigned the job of taking the first eleven and doing with us what he has to do, to run and prepare the most successful outfit that he possibly can. Like any team, corporation or army, two generals is always a quick course for disaster. Unless two generals have the closest of communication, problems are sure to evolve.

It would be fair to say that the communication hasn't been great and, as a result, the club is suffering. We haven't been playing great cricket, and I think as always happens, everyone is suddenly searching for the answers why. To me it is a great shame that there hasn't been a stronger bond between the new coach, who has worked harder than I have ever seen, and the senior players, who have had trouble taking on his methods.

How the relationship with Buck continues to evolve remains to be seen. I know that he has the support of the majority of the club, who are grasping his methodology eagerly. I just hope that with experience the coach/player relationship can continue to improve. No doubt Buck needs to adapt his style to the rigours of the county game, but that comes with experience and renewed wisdom. The county game is so vastly different to the Australian domestic competition that there needs to be flexibility, and I just hope that Buck is given the opportunity he needs to help Middlesex enjoy the glory days that they have been so used to in their rich history.

Friday, 31 July – foreign languages

Imagine my dilemma when I arrived in London to a completely foreign language. Obviously I wasn't listening to the same mystery lingo as if I had travelled to Germany, France or Italy, but I was experiencing extreme difficulty grasping the accents and parlance of a couple of my cockney-tongued London team-mates.

Phil Tufnell, Jason Pooley and Keith Dutch are particularly dicey on the old ears. Over the years, my auditory canals have been toughened up by various foreign languages. Having lived in Scotland for a summer, I thought my improved familiarity with fast-lipped Scotsmen would have prepared me for any alien pronunciations. Add to my Scottish stint six months of living with Hendy Springer, the Barbadian off-spinner, and I figured that I was well on my way to greater multi-lingual heights.

Unfortunately, my English summer with Middlesex may be leading me backwards in my journey to achieving a life goal of multi-linguality. Sure my team-mates speak English, but it is English with a difference. Commonly called cockney rhyming slang, I am having all sorts of trouble fully grasping their everyday chat. Take this morning for example. Phil Tufnell arrived at Lord's and without blinking or twitching a mickey-taking eyelid, he described for me yesterday's day off. I am curious whether it makes any sense to you. It went something like this:

JL, me ol' mate, I have to tell you a Jackanory about what 'appened yesterdey on me day orf. I woke up at me Mickey Mouse and, after a Ruby Murray, a few oily rags and 'alf a dozen Aristotles of lager last Snow White, I thought to me self 'Cor, you don't 'alf pen 'n' ink.' I was feeling 'orrible so I decided I couldn't 'alf do with a David Gower, a brush of the ol' Hampstead Heath and a good diggin' the grave.

After me David Gower and diggin' the grave, I put on me almond rocks, a brand new pair of Danny la Rues, a nice whistle 'n' flute, a new dickie dirt and a ridiculous red steak 'n' kidney pie which was a bit tight on me ol' Gregory Peck.

It was a lovely day and the ol' currant bun was shining with not a cloud in the apple pie, so I went down the apples and pears, jumped into me jam jar and took off down the frog 'n' toad to the Stacey Keech. Luckily, I had me Jackie Rowell lying on me front pound a meat so I might even 'ave meself a swim at the ol' Stacey.

Anyway, on the way to the Stacey Keech, the jam jar broke down so I had to take the ol' Frankie Laine. When I got down to the Stacey, I got straight on the dog 'n' bone and called a couple of me muckers who I told to forget the Stacey and meet me at the ol' rub a dub for a couple of swift halfs. While I was waiting for me muckers to arrive, I sat on the Stacey and admired the lovely thrupney bits and scotch eggs. Unfortunately, I sat too long in the currant bun and me ol' I suppose got burnt to a crisp.

Eventually, when me muckers arrived at the rub a dub, they said they were all boracic lint so all they'd be able to do was 'ave a butcher's hook at the ol' me 'n' you. I said don't worry boys, I'll pick up the Jack 'n' Jill, but when I looked in me sky rocket, I realised I was a little short of Arthur Ashe as I only had a Lady Godiva and a little bit of rifle range.

I decided to talk to a certain fridge 'n' freezer and ask him if he could lend me a lazy cock 'n' hen but little did I know this fridge 'n' freezer turned out to be ginger beer, wearing a terrible pair of Lionel Blairs and a dodgy syrup of figs.

My day wasn't going to electric fan, so after we finished our Aristotles we decided to sneak off for a Jimmy Riddle in the carzey. Instead of going to the carzey, we found the tradesmen's Martin Shaw and luckily me china plates' jam jar was waiting out the tin tack and we Alcatrazed back up the frog 'n' toad to the safety of me ol' Mickey Mouse. What a day!

Now you may think I am making this up, but I can assure you my cockney mates carry on like this day in, day out. Not only are the rhymes difficult, but spoken in Tuffers' accent, life gets even tougher. If you're not on your guard, you have little chance of understanding a word of conversation.

Quite appropriately, we are playing Sri Lanka today. To say my mind is in a muddle tonight is something of an understatement. After conversing with Tuffers and meeting Sri Lankans named D.R.M. Jayawardene, R.S. Kaluwitharana, U.C. Hathurusinghe, H.D.P.K. Dharmasena and M. Villavarayan, my brain is spinning out of multi-lingual control.

It is all part of the experience, but even so, a foreign language in London seems a little unfair, doesn't it? To even up the score, the boys left me tonight with a glossary of their terms. To help you understand a typical Phil Tufnell day off, here's an interpretation of the lingo.

Jackanory (story), Mickey Mouse (house), Ruby Murray (curry), oily rags (fags), Aristotles (bottles), Snow White (night), pen 'n' ink (stink), David Gower (shower), Hampstead Heath (teeth), diggin' the grave (shave), almond rocks (socks), Danny la Rues (shoes), whistle 'n' flute (suit), dickie dirt (shirt), steak 'n' kidney pie (tie), Gregory Peck (neck), currant bun (sun), apple pie (sky), apples 'n' pears (stairs), jam jar (car), frog 'n' toad (road), Stacey Keech (beach), Jackie Rowell (towel), pound a meat (seat), Frankie Laine (train), dog 'n' bone (phone), muckers (mates), rub a dub (pub), swift half (half a pint), thrupney bits (tits), scotch eggs (legs), I suppose (nose), boracic lint (skint), butcher's hook (look), me 'n' you (menu), Jack 'n' Jill (bill), sky rocket (pocket), Arthur Ashe (cash), Lady Godiva (fiver), rifle range (change), fridge 'n' freezer (geezer), cock 'n' hen (ten), ginger beer (queer), Lionel Blairs (flares), syrup of figs (wig), electric fan (plan), Jimmy Riddle (piddle), carzey (toilet), Martin Shaw (door), china plates (mates), tin tack (back), Alcatrazed (escaped).

To all you connoisseurs of rhyming slang, you'll have to excuse me if I haven't got it exactly right.

PS I saw a great century by David Goodchild today, hopefully his first of many.

Sunday, 2 August – the world champions in town

Atapattu, Jayasuriya, Jayawardene, Kaluwitharana and Hathurusinghe – not only tricky names to pronounce but also tricky players to stop when thrashing their cricket bats at the bruised and battered leather projectile commonly known as a cricket ball. Straight drives, fierce pull and cut shots and cheeky running between the wickets makes these current world champions as difficult to contain as an avalanche in a snowfield.

Without being outright sloggers, every one of the top seven batsmen seems to turn over the run-rate as effortlessly as Michael Owen scores World Cup goals. Not many players can boast of having transformed the game of cricket like Jayasuriya and Kaluwitharana have done to the one-day game. Both of these batting dynamos, all five foot four of them, can rightfully claim to have made a significant mark on the changing approach to the shorter version of the game. It was these two 'thrashing machines' who arguably introduced the strategy of belting opening bowlers from ball one of a one-day affair. By following the theory that there is more room in the air than on the ground, they revolutionised the way teams are taking advantage of the first fifteen overs of one-day cricket. It is almost commonplace now for international, county, even club cricket teams to opt for the ultra-aggressive opening batsmen in their one-day outfit. Alistair Brown, Nick Knight, Adam Gilchrist, Mark Waugh, Michael Di Venuto and Sachin Tendulkar do it for their countries; Robert Croft and Ryan Campbell do it for their first-class sides; and Peter Gardiner does it for the Scarborough firsts in downtown Perth grade cricket. It seems to be the way to go these days, leaving blockers like myself to clean up the scraps and push the singles when the field has spread after fifteen overs!

Refreshingly, the Sri Lankans boldly adopt as positive an approach to the first-class game as they do to the one-dayers. They play a wonderfully entertaining style of cricket, not only in their batting and fielding but also in the way they go about their business. There is never a shortage of laughing and smiling on the field as they punish and take advantage of any delivery that's even the slightest bit on the loose side. The regularity of boundaries hit over the last two days at Lord's was terrific to see.

The ratio of balls faced to boundaries scored, without knowing a figure, must have sent Middlesex scorer M.J. Smith into something of a frenzy up in the Lord's scorer's box. Not only were his pencils becoming blunter with every delightful Sri Lankan plunder, but I also noticed the umpires leaving Lord's tonight with their arms in slings – obviously as a result of signalling such an extraordinary number of boundaries throughout the day.

Yesterday, acting captain Jayasuriya played shots which would have Geoffrey Boycott shaking his head in disbelief. One stroke, a mis-timed flick over midwicket, ended up crashing one bounce into the deep-point advertising boards – an extraordinary shot from an extraordinary player. Although he scored only 20-odd runs, his short stay at the crease was like watching Hulk Hogan arm wrestle King Kong Bundy – short in duration, but filled with the power play and brutal force of such an eventful match-up.

His opening partner was Marvan Atapattu. What a class act! A man with the unenviable record of one run in his first six Test innings, he was as technically correct as any text book may preach, yet his ability to play fierce strokes all around the wicket was amazing to watch. He timed the ball as sweetly as anything in scoring a magnificently entertaining first-class century.

Hashan Tillekeratne, the chirpy left-hander, missed out today, but his mates Kaluwitharana and Jayawardene, tiny in stature, giants in ability, played innings of rare touch and quality. How men who are no taller than Danny DeVito, with arms as thin as raw spaghetti, can hit the ball as hard and as precisely as they do is beyond my comprehension. Their bats look massive in their hands, yet they use them more like a magician's wand than a caveman's club.

Come The Oval Test match in a few weeks' time, the Sri Lankans may lack a little fire power in their bowling attack, but I can assure you their batting line-up will be worth paying your hard-earned cash to go and see. The scary part of our current encounter is the absence of batting masters Aravinda de Silva and Arjuna Ranatunga. The English Test and one-day teams should take note. Today's batting order is excellent – awesome is the only way to describe a full-strength Sri Lankan line-up.

It may sound odd that I am praising the opposition so highly in the middle of a game, but in a funny sort of way, I have thoroughly enjoyed watching these guys batting for the last 110 overs. They play the game the way it should be played. Rod Marsh once told me that 'batting is about scoring runs. It doesn't matter how long you stay in the middle. At the end of the day, it is the runs that matter.' These Sri Lankans adopt this approach, entertaining the crowd for one thing and also giving their bowlers plenty of time to bowl out their opponents. It is hardly surprising that they hold the record for the highest aggregate team score in a Test match. I wouldn't have minded being a spectator on that fateful day, perhaps not from the slips like today, but rather from the grandstand enjoying the pleasures of assassins batting at their best.

Considering the one-off Test match between Sri Lanka and England is to be played at The Oval in a fortnight, the odds on Sri Lanka are very quickly shortening. Surrey have been dominant in the County Championship this season, thanks to spinners Saqlain Mushtaq and Ian Salisbury. If the history of The Oval pitch is anything to go by, England may well be in for as tough a Test match as any they have played against South Africa this summer. Once again, time will tell!

Monday, 3 August – that weather again!

Call it Ollie Ozone layer. Call it Eric El Niño. Call it Gloria Global Warming. Even just call it Barry Bad Luck. In other words, call it whatever you want, but all I know is that this crazy changing of the world's climate is simply preposterous.

Yet another day was rain-affected, leaving us with yet another day of changing-room boredom and yet another frustratingly resultless fixture against the international tourists. Folk from the Lord's groundstaff and catering fraternity, from the London bus drivers to the local Indian newsagent, from the corner fish 'n' chip cook to the BBC news readers are all singing an identical chorus. 'I can't remember a summer like this for years. It's been horrible. It is usually so beautiful this time of the year. It is not always like this you know!'

I am hearing it everywhere I go and not only because I am a cricketer, but because I am now a London local. The whole country seems to be in mourning over the persistent rain and lack of 'sun, glorious sun'. But England is not the only place suffering. Antonio, the local hairdresser, after his standard complaints about the last few months' weather, told me about the horrific temperatures and summer bush fires in his hometown of Athens. The 110-degree temperatures have devastated his family who live just outside the Greek capital.

'Justin, I just a can'ta work it out. Humans think they have a all the answers, but I have a funny a feeling the world is coming to an end, just like it says in the Bible. They keepa cutting down alla the trees, it worries me, my friend, it really worries me.'

The nervous Greek hairdresser, shaking with distress, nearly cut off my ears as he passionately put across his point of view. He definitely has a point; something is surely amiss. Not least of all my left ear.

Even Perth, usually mild in the winters, is experiencing zero-degree mornings. Every time I ring home, the talk of the town is the freezing cold winter they are all trying to come to terms with. Over the phone I can nearly hear my mum's teeth chattering in protest at the strange conditions, more like Finland than Western Australia.

The Miami heatwaves, the Papua New Guinea tidal waves, the Chinese floods, the hole in the ozone layer and the number of abandoned days in county cricket, all proof, at differing scales of course, that the world is in a state of transformation.

Driving home from Lord's tonight I was most distressed to have to turn on the headlights in my car. Considering the clock had just ticked over to 6.30 p.m. the horrible realisation that the summer was coming to an abrupt end suddenly dawned upon me. Where is that wonderful English summer twilight period where you can leave the pub at night only to be greeted by clear bright skies and fresh dry evening air?

Keith Brown, Middlesex's most senior player apart from Mike Gatting, commented at lunchtime today how quickly this summer has gone by. In fact, it seems like only yesterday that I arrived in London for the start of the county season. In many respects the season has felt a little bit like a rollercoaster ride on Brighton pier. You line up for what seems an eternity, eventually you buckle in for the ride and then, before you know it, you have experienced a quick thrill and you're walking towards the ice-cream van wondering where the adrenalin of the ride had disappeared to.

The wet summer has taken away much of the momentum and expectation of the county season. Relatively speaking, it isn't half as devastating as the other things suffering from the changing climate, but from this Aussie's point of view the rain is driving me potty. No one is losing their houses or lives as a result of the continued English rain, but I have to say I am losing my hair as fast as Allan Donald bowls his spine-tingling bumper. Not as a result of Antonio the Greek hairdresser's shaky right hand but rather due to the psychotic habit I have acquired of pulling it out every time I sit and watch this rain fall from the bleak, grey London skies.

Another rainy day and I might end up in the nut house. Tomorrow is supposed to be the start of the 'real' summer. The *Big Breakfast* weather crew promise us that the next week will be dry and hot, and more like the English summer we have all been looking forward to. I won't hold my breath, but my fingers and toes are all crossed.

Imagine my added frustration when I read an article in this morning's paper, headed 'Hottest Month Fuels

Fear on Global Warming'. Reports from the USA say that the average temperature worldwide in July was 16.5°C, about 0.7°C above normal for July. This was 0.3°C higher than the previous hottest month – July last year. The year had also begun with the warmest January since records began.

Can you imagine, here's me, a whingeing Aussie, complaining about the weather and in fact everywhere else in the world is as hot and dry as it's ever been. It's like hearing about Bill Gates' huge fortune and wishing he would donate 0.1 per cent of it to your personal bank balance. If it is so hot around the world I am sure a few of the hotter countries would be only too happy to donate a few degrees of warmth to England. We are only asking for a small percentage of their heat to brighten up this particular English summer. I am sure, like a Bill Gates donation, a small change in the weather would surely bring a big smile to this once sun-tanned face of mine.

CHAPTER TWELVE

Heroes

Wednesday, 5 August – the Brian Lara storm

A haunting whisper has been making its way through county cricket over the last few months. 'Somebody is going to pay. Somebody is really going to pay. When it comes it is going to be ugly, it's going to big, it's going to be a monster. I just hope it isn't us who gets in the way of the inevitable storm.'

Every county has joked about the daunting prospect, but unfortunately it was Middlesex who today copped the hurricane that has been brewing ominously for the last four months. This hurricane, of course, was in the form of one B.C. Lara. After a disappointing season, with the bat and the authorities (if the paper is anything to go by), Brian Lara proved to all his detractors why he is one of the world's greatest batsmen. At stumps the West Indian and Warwickshire captain is a magnificent 225 not out. Although the Lord's pitch is a belter, his innings was simply awesome. Technically he was as close to batting perfection as one can achieve and his application, under growing internal and external pressure, was outstandingly admirable.

The way he went about his innings was, painfully,

a pleasure to watch. In the changing-rooms tonight, John Buchanan told me that in all his coaching career he has never witnessed a batting 'wagon wheel' like he saw today. A boundary was scored to almost every part of the ground. Most players score their runs in certain areas but today the computer chart showed an innings of lines all around the wicket. A tribute to Brian Lara's incredible ability and natural strokeplay.

One of the most refreshing aspects of the way he played was the sheer simplicity of his game. If you didn't know the left-hander in the centre of Lord's was B.C. Lara you could have easily mistaken him for any first-class, even village, cricketer. That is, only in the way he looked of course. He walked onto cricket's Mecca wearing a pair of spikeless running shoes. His protective equipment included a pair of anonymous pads and gloves, a stickerless bat with a blue scoop in its spine and a blue Warwickshire helmet. Although he may have looked anonymous, the West Indian dynamo's feet danced like Michael Flatley's, as he flayed the ball to every part of Lord's. It really was brilliant.

As he cruised past a century, in 130 balls, a distinct memory flooded my mind. Playing golf in Alice Springs last year he gave me a tip about batting. 'JL, when you're having a good day you have to make sure you cash in and have a great day. There is a lot of days when you miss out, so when you get set you have to make sure you get yourself a really big score.'

This advice has helped me in my batting exploits but it also caused me a migraine headache standing in the long-overdue sunshine today. Knowing his appetite for his trademark double, triple and even quintuple centuries, we may not have seen the last of Lara in this innings. It was almost as if the blue skies and sunshine thawed out his feet, arms and bat as he went on a warpath of destruction on my team-mate bowlers. A pleasure to watch for any cricket purist who enjoys destruction at its best.

This week I have feasted on some incredible batsmanship. Unfortunately I have been watching from the slips, but between Lara today and the Sri Lankans earlier in the week I have seen some awesome stuff. I wonder how long he will go on for tomorrow? I have a feeling this could be big, even bigger than the rumour expected! By the look in his eye he will be in no mood for generosity. His batting philosophy is beating mercilessly in my ears and throbbing feet. We will wait and see, tomorrow is another day. You just never know.

Saturday, 8 August – I have seen it all

It isn't the first time, and I am certain it won't be the last time, that incidents in a game of cricket have me shaking my head in bewilderment, leaving me laughing on the inside, and marvelling at the great mysteries of the best game in the world. Over the last two days 'the game' has flexed its muscles and reminded all involved, in a strong booming voice, 'Never take me for granted. When you think you have me mastered, you had better think again because I always have a trick up my sleeve to test your humour and fortitude.'

Day two, Middlesex versus Warwickshire at Lord's, a fairly routine county affair, although B.C. Lara just happened to be walking to the middle with 225 runs to his name. Considering that yesterday he batted like a man as hungry for runs as a lean hyena is for meat, the prospects for this morning looked as grim as the proverbial reaper. Surely Lara was prepared to threaten his previous batting world record. The look in his eye as he swaggered to the crease was ominous, almost cheeky, as he had his opposition, the crowd and the story-craving media gasping in expectation for what was about to unfold.

Extraordinarily, the second over of the morning produced an inswinger from Richard Johnson, which magically trapped the West Indian maestro adjacently in front of all three stumps. From slips, Keith Brown, Mike Gatting and I were trampoline jumping and attempting somersaults in a bid to receive a positive response from umpire John Harris. Fortunately, the umpire's rising right finger ordered B.C. Lara back to the pavilion for a well-earned rest, while yours truly and my leg-weary team-mates gleefully celebrated the dismissal, relieved as much as jubilant, with high fives, hugs and backslapping. Admittedly his innings was entertaining, but enough was enough, and the sight of his backside was almost as pleasant as seeing Elle McPherson cat-walking back to the Lord's pavilion in a lacy g-string.

The surprising exit of Brian Lara triggered off a very humorous sequence of events, which reinforced the old saying 'all in a day's cricket'. Three overs after Lara's dismissal, Neil Smith, a born and bred county slogger, who hits sixes for a pastime, crashed a ball from a Tuffers slower, loopier delivery straight into the back of David Nash who was standing in the way at short leg. Smith hit the ball as hard as a Holyfield right hook, and by the way Nashy hit the deck he might as well have been on the end of the heavyweight champion's knockout blow. You could have mistaken Nashy's fall for an assassination attempt as he rolled around the Lord's turf like a football player rolls around after being tripped in the penalty area.

Due to the roundness of Nashy's trunk area, the ball ballooned to mid-on where Paul Weekes accepted the easiest of catches. As is tradition, Nashy's ten team-mates, initially expressing limited concern, spent the next few minutes laughing themselves senseless as the little battler hobbled off with the physio to ice up his bruised ribs. It always amazes me how an injured player always seems to limp off even if it isn't his leg that has been hurt. Ever the sceptic!

As for Smith, he also bent over the assassinated Nash, but when he realised that he was out for his troubles, he quickly lost interest and proceeded to curse his misfortune all the way back to his bench seat in the visitors' changing-rooms.

During our innings, as fast bowler Ed Giddins took the second new ball, Tuffers found himself almost in a state of panic, as he couldn't seem to keep himself awake. 'I knew I shouldn't 'ave 'ad that extra lamb chop at lunch. You know what I mean. I am an idiot; you know what I mean. I should know better, you know what I mean, but I wasn't expectin' to bat today, mate. You know what I mean, mate, I just can't keep me mince pies open. You know what I mean. This is terrible, what if I fall asleep when Giddins is bowling to me, you know what I mean, I'll be dead meat mate, you know what I mean.'

Sitting in his corner, he drank mugs of coffee and smoked more and more fags as he tried to wake himself up. He splashed water over his face, had himself a cold shower, even tried to dance his way out of his dilemma as he turned the CD player on full bore. Panic was turning to grief as yet another Middlesex wicket fell.

'That extra lamb chop does it every time, you know what I mean, it was that extra, bloody lamb chop. Phys, you have to help me mate. Have you got any smelling salts? You know what I mean, I need some smelling salts mate, I need some smelling salts, what if I fall asleep mate, you know what I mean, Giddins will kill me mate. Little Poppy [his daughter] mate, you know what I mean, phys, I can't die on the cricket field mate, you know what I mean, little Poppy mate, I can't die on the cricket field because I can't keep my eyes open mate. You know what I mean.'

Smelling salts? I couldn't believe my ears, but as my eyes filled with hysterical tears Tuffers looked at me with the most serious of intent.

'JL mate, don't laugh mate, you know what I mean, I just can't keep awake mate, you know what I mean, I don't know what to do mate, what if I'm still feeling like this when I get out to the middle mate. Browny might as well declare, you know what I mean. I know we haven't avoided the follow-on but I can't bat when me mince pies refuse to stay open, you know what I mean mate, you know what I mean.'

Tuffers eventually trudged to the crease and taking my advice swung his arms a few times, ran on the spot and skipped around the crease before facing his first ball. Unsurprisingly, his attempted cover drive rocketed into his left foot before rolling onto the stumps and within a few minutes he was back in the rooms with a golden duck to his name.

'You know what I mean, I got out there and felt fine mate, you know what I mean. I was feeling awake, but I think my bat just didn't come through straight, you know what I mean. I don't know what all the worry was about, you know what I mean. Sorry guys, you know what I mean, a bloody duck, sorry guys it was that extra bloody lamb chop. Extra lamb chops at lunch, stopped me getting my feet moving, you know what I mean. Sorry guys.'

I had heard it all but at least it helped cheer us all up after the last few days. First it was Brian Lara's destruction, then while I was batting I was cruising along before Ashley Giles, England's latest left-arm spinner, dismissed me in the most bizarre circumstances. Bowling into the rough outside my off stump, a ball bounced viciously and hit me on the shoulder. From my now bruised shoulder the ball flew into the air before dropping into the same rough patch that Ashley had been aiming at all afternoon. After reaching the turf, the ball then spun back underneath my feet and, as I turned to find the guided missile, I accidentally kicked it back towards my stumps. Much to my horror, my aim was as good as a Michael Owen strike and as a consequence my bails were sent flying, in turn sending me on my sad and sorry way. Again I had never seen anything like it!

They say it's all in a day's cricket, hence the infatuation with the game. You just never know what it has up its sleeve to test its willing competitors.

Monday, 10 August – England beat the South Africans

Twelve years is a long time to wait for a Test series victory, so I am sure the England team will make the most of today's magnificent conquest of South Africa. At 11.00 a.m. this morning the game was set for a thriller. The visitors had 33 runs to score, England just two wickets to secure.

Test cricket is tense at the best of times, but on this overcast morning a game could hardly have been tenser. Considering the whole series relied on the outcome of these two targets, there were very few long fingernails left on millions of fingers around the country, or for that matter around South Africa. One thing's for sure, there will have been a few sleepless bodies and drained minds arriving at Headingley at 9.00 a.m. this morning. Every possible scenario will have run through the brains of each person involved in this Test match. Between them, players, coaches, managers and spectators will have dreamed up all the possible permutations. Two wickets in the first two balls? Batsman Shaun Pollock smashing a quick-fire 30 to take his team to victory? A rain-abandoned day? The prospect of the new ball ruining the South African hopes? Allan Donald boldly holding on with Pollock for a fighting and frustrating victory? Gus Fraser taking another five wickets and another man-of-the-match award for his triumphant team? England dropping crucial catches and falling short again? A couple of poor umpiring decisions to go one team's way? Debutant Ntini hooking a six for an unlikely victory?

So much speculation, so many of the dreaded 'what

ifs?', so many useless questions, all blown out of the water and answered within half an hour's play this morning. It is fascinating the games that can be invented and played in your imagination.

As it turned out, the script couldn't have been more perfect for home-town hero Darren Gough as he trapped Ntini lbw on his beloved Headingley turf. With a roaring Gough appeal and a successful umpiring adjudication, at 11.30 it was game over. For the whole of the England team and its patriotic supporters, it must have been an incredible feeling – victory was now a reality, rather than a hopeful ambition.

Game, set and match, as they say at the end of a tennis match. Alec Stewart's team has finally blasted off the reputation of finishing so close yet so far. 'What might have been' has at last been replaced with 'what is'; and 'what is' is a resurgence of an English cricket team which has a core of very good players who look set to make an impact on the world stage.

The approaching Ashes series now takes on a different look. Suddenly we, the Australians, are up against a talented team full of players who believe they can win games of Test cricket. They have just proved to themselves that they have what it takes to beat a very tough and disciplined team like South Africa. With belief, a talented team of players becomes an ominous outfit. As losing becomes a habit, so does winning. To fight back and win the last two Tests is a feat in itself, but to fight back and win two live rubbers to secure a Test series is an even greater achievement.

Brian Lara said to me at Lord's on Thursday morning that he hoped England win this series 'for the sake of cricket'. He is probably right, as now the England Test team can be seen as a seriously competitive force in the international arena. Obviously, one series result doesn't erase the last twelve years, but at least it sets them back on the right path.

Not only is today's result a bonus for international cricket, but it is also a major plus for the English domestic game. So much has been said about English cricket and the perceived dwindling of public interest in and support for Test and county games. There is no doubt in my mind that continued success by the Test team will have a massively positive effect upon the perception of the game of cricket as a whole.

A successful Test team is the breeding ground for heroes, and it is heroes in our society who help make a sport attractive to the public. Through the emotions they generate, in children and adults, they conjure up support and interest. Heroes are crucial to the game. Just as David Beckham, Michael Owen and Alan Shearer are heroes in the football world, cricket needs men like Darren Gough, Alec Stewart, Mark Ramprakash and Angus Fraser to step up and become heroes and role models for the younger generation of aspiring cricketers. Then little Johnny or schoolboy Goughy will want to play the game and one day play for their country. This is the only way for the game to develop and prosper.

The old adage that 'winners are grinners' is not only appropriate for the players involved in a victory, it is especially relevant for the supporters who are so crucial to the game. People like to see winners, they like success, and the more of it that they can get the happier they will be. In fact, the happier everybody will be.

Today England cricket is revelling in its national

heroes. That has to be healthy for their game, which really is a national treasure. In this fickle world, even a national treasure dear to the hearts of so many can be lost to cynicism, sheer disappointment and frustration. For a relatively short time in the enormously rich history of English cricket, the heart of the game may have been forgotten, purely because there hasn't been all that much for the public, even the most patriotic, to sing and grin about.

Here's cheers to the England Test team today! The more they win, the more the game will blossom. It is just a shame their next port of call is the Ashes in Australia, where the game of cricket and its heroes are blossoming like summer roses. The challenge is now on for today's English heroes.

CHAPTER THIRTEEN
Unlucky for Some

Tuesday, 11 August – living in London

What a morning! My day today was similar to *Nightmare on Elm Street I, II* and *III*. The only difference was that this was a real-life nightmare and I didn't have the option of opening my eyes for instant relief from those Freddy Krueger spirits haunting my brain. It wasn't my bedsheets that ended up soaking wet with terrified perspiration, but rather three changes of clothing that were ruined in the rush before we had even reached a quiet, lunchtime cup of tea.

After an entertaining evening in the Lord's Tavern with Brian Lara, I found myself returning to Lord's early this morning to pick up my car from cricket headquarters. It was foolishly decided last night that the best way to avoid a potential hangover was to enjoy an early-morning, easy, therapeutic jog from my flat back to Lord's to retrieve my abandoned car. I guess it would have been even more foolish to drive my car home last night with half a dozen pints of Foster's under my belt, but that is a different story.

Fighting my good intentions, I eventually tore myself from my warm bed and at 6.45 a.m. pulled on a pair of running shoes and shorts, and snuck out of my London abode to make the short journey down West End Lane and Abbey Road to a yawning Lord's cricket ground. Still wiping the sleep from my eyes, I experienced 'Nightmare on West End Lane 1'.

As I jogged along West Hampstead's quiet main road, I stared in terror as an older man, carrying a large silver briefcase, came running towards me shouting, 'I am going to kill you, you bastard, I am going to kill you.' If I wasn't awake before, I certainly was now as the 'fight or flight' adrenal glands worked overtime to save me from what I thought would be my last breathing moment.

Tensing myself as though I was just about to be tackled by Jonah Lomu, I ran straight towards him like William Wallace in a battlefield scene from *Braveheart*. Fortunately, as we were about to collide, he seemed to fake a dummy and fell flat on the footpath. I ran on leaving him sprawled out on all fours, shouting more obscenities and death threats.

I have absolutely no idea what the incident was all about, but I do know that the next kilometre of easy jogging was replaced by a thousand metres of Carl Lewis-style sprint work. Never before have I felt the hair stand up on the back of my neck like it did this morning. When I arrived at Lord's, I was sweating like a man just out of a sauna, even though the air was chilly and crisp, and I was shaking like a baby's rattle.

I have always thought that there are a few strange characters walking around the streets of London but this guy has to take the cake. An odd-looking man in his mid forties, he was wearing a pair of beltless suit trousers with a white crumpled T-shirt. His hair was long, but brushed, and I think he looked reasonably clean-shaven. The briefcase looked like the type that an assassin may carry. Why he picked me as his early-morning target remains a mystery. Maybe he had heard I was hungry to score mountains of runs in the upcoming Ashes battle and he wanted to do his part for his country; or maybe he just doesn't like Aussies. Who knows? More realistically, he had probably just had a session on cocaine or speed and I happened to be the first person he ran into after his last hit. Bad luck for me but at least I was still alive to live out 'Nightmare on Woodhouse Road 2'.

After recovering from the early-morning attack by the would-be Aussie assassin, it was off to one of life's scariest institutions for round two of today's real-life nightmare. I drove to Woodhouse Lane, Finchley, for what was sure to be a terribly uncomfortable experience. I had been putting it off for months, maybe even years. This is something that leaves me more fearful than facing Curtly Ambrose without my pads or protective box. Nothing can be worse than that I hear you say, but I promise you, a visit to the London Day Surgery is at the top of my list of greatest fears.

I, probably like you, have hated dentists since my first-ever visit as a little boy. The sterile smell, the needles and the churning drill noises all add to the horror of one of life's miseries. Today I was there to have an old root removed from the socket that used to be the home of my right eyetooth (extracted in June). After pumping myself up for the event I pressed the intercom button which unlocked the door to the surgery. After making my way up the creaking staircase, I pushed my way through the tinted door and was greeted by a smiling receptionist. Pleasant as she was to start with, the greeting abruptly changed tone. Within a minute or so, she had only added to the pain that I was about to endure by politely asking me to pay the bill before having the operation. Not only was the account big enough to feed a family for a year, but I was starting to question why I was paying the bill before the treatment. Did they know something I didn't? Was there a chance that I wouldn't come out of it alive? Was I being irrational?

After signing an astronomically large cheque I was led into the sterile operating theatre. If I had harboured any thoughts of relaxing before the procedure, they were quickly dispelled. The surgeon, wielding a needle the size of a mini cricket bat and playing the *Mission Impossible* theme tune on his stereo system, jabbed and prodded and eventually numbed the infected area. With music blaring in the background and bright lights blurring my vision, all I could feel for the next twenty minutes was the crunching of bone and ripping of flesh as he successfully detached the eyetooth root from my war-stricken gum.

As the ripping and grinding continued, the music seemed to get louder and the surgeon played out his role as a mad doctor in a James Bond movie. Cringe, cringe, cringe! The hair on the back of my neck was again standing on end and my eyeballs were rolling around as I seemed to lurch in and out of sanity. I felt like jumping out of the chair and running away, but I had no energy left in my legs after sprinting a kilometre down West End Lane earlier in the morning.

When the operation came to an end, the dentist, now transformed in my mind to some sort of crazed psychopath, simply smiled and sent me on my merry way. I survived the trauma, but I wouldn't be surprised if I am never the same again. In less than six waking hours today I could have been psychologically scarred for life, thanks to a black-haired, English dental surgeon driving a semi-trailer through my bleeding gums and his assassin mate on West End Lane. As I drove home to the sympathy of my wife and daughter, I was sure that the remainder of the day could only look up. Wrong again!

Nightmare on Lyncroft Gardens 3: after two traumas in one day, what's one more to add to the misery? With swollen lips and gums, pumping headache, and in financial tatters, I drove home and double-parked my car outside the flat. You may call it lazy, but the longer I have been in London the more this has become a normality in the daily routine of living and parking. After parking the car as close as I could to the parked car on the verge, I slowly walked up to the front door and rang the bell. With a click, the door unlocked and let me through to our staircase. Before I reached my second-storey front door . . . BANG!! Beep, Beep, Beep! An alarm was screaming, going mental outside our flat.

Surely it couldn't be? It was! A minicab driver, looking on the opposite side of the street, crashed straight into the back of my car, smashing the back lights into a thousand pieces. Obviously it was his fault, and obviously it was lucky no one was in the car at the time, but still, what a pain in the backside.

Insurance claims, panel beating, explanations to my car sponsor loomed – all the things you don't need, especially today, when my nerves were already reduced to the width of a piece of dental floss. I didn't even have the energy to argue with the taxi driver who was very apologetic and upset. Sue and Jessica had come rushing down to see what the matter was and after exchanging the relevant information, I carried Jessica back upstairs and fell on to the couch where I didn't move for the rest of the day. I wasn't game!

They say you learn something every day. At least when I go to bed tonight, I will be able to handle the most vivid of nightmares no matter how gruesome they become. There is nowhere to hide when the nightmares are actually happening in your waking hours. Surely tomorrow will be more fruitful?

Wednesday, 12 August – Langer's guide to England holidays

A glass of 1983 Château Pichon-Longueville, Comtesse de Lalande, a dozen crisp, green asparagus spears followed by smoked salmon, roast chicken and a platter of fresh raspberries and strawberries. All freshly grown and prepared with the love and mastery of your grandmother's hand. A perfect way to celebrate two days off the county cricket circuit.

This isn't a traveller's guide to wining and dining through England but I have to say, if you are looking for a relaxing couple of days, I can highly recommend the South West of England, particularly the lovely Deer Park Hotel in Honiton, Devon. It is the perfect escape from a hectic London lifestyle. Great food, fine wine and service usually reserved for a week of spoiling from your own mum. The country air is so fresh you can nearly feel your lungs sitting inside your chest, hands behind their head, feet up, enjoying the break from the heavily polluted London air. Built on a huge property, away from the motorways, the green fields and lush lawns are therapy in themselves. Fresh air, running streams and singing birds add to the allure of a lifestyle that can only accelerate the reduction of any inflated stress levels and help in making the morning alarm clock seem less of an enemy intruder in your bedroom.

After a month of solid county cricket, with only a couple of rest days in between new games, I must admit the nerves tend to become a little frayed and getting out of bed of a morning becomes more of a chore than earlier in the season. On Sunday morning while having breakfast with Gatt and Ramps I asked them: 'Is it just me, or is it getting harder to pull yourself out of bed every morning?'

At this they looked at each other, smiled and replied, 'Get used to it, pal, that's how we feel every single county season.'

Conversation closed, as the respect for each other's aching backs, legs and brains needed no more comment.

I was keen at the start of the season to keep on top of this fatigue factor but I have to admit county cricket is a lot more tiring than I ever imagined. It is a longer season, in relation to quantity of cricket, than I have ever experienced before and it does take its toll no matter how hard you try to manage your body and mind.

One way of easing the cumulative fatigue is an escape at every opportunity. An escape from my cricket bat, an escape from my team-mates, an escape from the changing-room and an escape from morning warm-ups. If you don't do it, you start seeing cricket balls in your sleep, not a healthy existence even for the greatest of cricket lovers. Thank God for retreats like this one.

Saturday, 15 August – sinking of the *Titanic*!

'Sussex by the Sea' – my abiding memory of today. The gentleman in the crowd singing this famous tune could be mistaken for Luciano Pavarotti when he booms his short chorus at different intervals throughout a day's play. His operatic voice encourages loud applause from the Sussex supporters who lap up the atmosphere in the fresh sea air, a luxury provided free of charge by the Sussex County Cricket Club.

Hove cricket ground is a wonderful place to play cricket, that is of course unless you're a Middlesex county cricketer in 1998. We have had about as much success at Hove this summer as David Beckham has had with the English football crowds since returning from the World Cup. A few weeks ago, we were bowled out for a paltry score of 120 in the Sunday League game under the new Sussex lights. An ordinary performance then, on a traditionally flat Hove wicket.

When we arrived yesterday morning, it was impossible to see the cut pitch when you were sitting in the pavilion. The grass was so lush and green on our playing facility that the only distinguishing features between the pitch and the outfield were four white lines painted twenty-two yards apart. I was staggered that we were about to commence a first-class game on a surface resembling the thick lawn in my backyard. I had heard of playing on green seaming pitches in England, but this was really taking it to the extreme. The whisper was that they had to leave it grassy, or it simply played too flat, low and very slow. After initial inspection, I think we would have settled for one of those low slow ones thanks. Instead it looked like the opening batsmen would be walking to the gallows rather than out to the middle of the Sussex Cricket Club's playing surface.

At Nottingham I learnt a lesson in reading a cricket pitch, and I should have remembered about judging a book by its cover. When Sussex captain Chris Adams won the toss and batted, I, like the rest of my team-mates, almost fell off my chair with sheer delight and disbelief. 'He must be out of his bloody mind' was the general reaction that summed up the atmosphere in our changing-room. Being a bit of a sceptic, I started scratching my chin and thinking that there must be more to this decision than at first met the eye. Either Adams had experienced a moment of madness, or did he know something we didn't? Perhaps Adams was embarrassed about this pitch and figured the only way to dispel all the talk was to lead from the front and bat first. Maybe he knew that this deathly-looking thing wasn't going to be as bad as its appearance may have suggested.

He was right! He smashed 170 in as many balls, a magnificent innings of sheer bludgeoning of our inexperienced attack. Forget Vivian Richards, Chris Adams was as ruthless on our bowlers as the greatest of attackers could ever have been. To every part of the playing field he belted the ball as if he had a deeply rooted vendetta against it. His top-order men, including my Australian counterpart Michael Bevan, helped out the Sussex captain, and at stumps the home side were 360 for 7, an extraordinary effort on a pitch that could quite easily have been written off as a batsman's worst nightmare.

Today, we started off with a bang, dismissing the final three Sussex batsmen within half an hour of play. As the final wickets fell our spirits, after our first-day hammering, were momentarily lifted. This was a promising start to the day, even if the pitch seemed to have dried out a little, and the ball, alarmingly, seemed to be hitting the wicketkeeper's gloves with more steam than it had all day yesterday. Walking off the field, the feeling in the team had picked up; maybe yesterday was just a bad day. I'm afraid not!

If day one was like a visit to the doctor-type bad day, today was more like the *Titanic* of bad days. Disaster struck the Middlesex County Cricket Club as we embarrassingly proceeded to lose twenty wickets in less than five hours, losing the championship game in less than two days. A sad day for Middlesex cricket! Bowled out once in a day is never good, bowled out twice is deplorable.

Coach John Buchanan was shattered, as you would expect. He has been working so hard to get this team back into the winning mode and yet we seem to be going from bad to worse. I guess the only remedy is hard work and that begins tomorrow at 9.00 a.m. – John has called for a centre-wicket training session at Hove. My team-mates are calling them 'bad boy nets'; I'd call them 'back to basics nets', or even 'save us from embarrassment again nets'.

Today was a shocker!

Sunday, 16 August – bad boy nets

Rather than spending today as day three against Sussex, we instead embarked upon a marathon training session geared towards polishing up the basics that seem to be eluding us at present. The boys' joke name suggests they are regarded as punishment for a poor performance. In a way, five hours of centre-wicket practice could be seen as this, but I get the feeling there is a lot more to it than that. John Buchanan, a perfectionist who is passionate about his team's performance, is more concerned about seeing an overall improvement than purely punishing his charges for the last two days' poor play.

Losing like we just have shouldn't be taken lightly, and although it would be easy to write off a poor game as just a bad couple of days, there is generally more to it than that. Analysing our mediocre performances over the last month is enough to drive you crazy; it is certainly driving our coach to a point of madness.

Maybe I could put our sub-standard showing in this match down to the summer holiday spirit in Brighton. The magnificent Brighton esplanade, the festivities on the famous Brighton Pier and the beachside bars and cafés, not to mention the bikini-clad visitors, all act as attractive deterrents to the task at hand on the field. Coincidentally, the sun has shone every day we've been in Brighton – an off-field trap for even the most dedicated of county cricketers. They also tell me that Brighton is the gay capital of Europe, although I'm quite sure that didn't have any effect on any of our players.

We could have done worse than substitute our performance at Hove with that of the women cricketers playing an Ashes second Test match at Worcester this week. We could have used a few of the massive batting scores which have dominated their Test series. The old Aussie saying, 'you're playing like a bunch of old girls', summed up our efforts on our last two journeys to Hove. I have to say it was very embarrassing being a part of both débâcles.

The Sussex pub was the escape route for our sorry, die-hard supporters who are also at their wits' end looking for reasons for our recent demise. The more beer they drank, the closer they came to dispelling the demons of disbelief which were invading their cricket well-being.

Maybe hitting the bottle is the way to go to pull us out of this trough? Then again, I think the hard work approach will be the better answer.

Apart from our poor performances against an improving Sussex team, it looks like Sussex's marketing initiatives have successfully attracted grand and encouraging numbers of home-town supporters this season. Through positive initiatives, like renaming the team 'The Sussex Sharks', the club has a new identity that helps freshen up their look on the county cricket roadshow. Sussex seem to be leading the way in promoting their team, the club and English domestic cricket.

In Australia, the naming and branding of the state teams has helped improve the image of the game and its players, opening up a greater marketplace for potential supporter and sponsor bases. Sussex have adopted this approach, with clever advertising and a polished image, which is so important for the life of the domestic game, and it is through the clubs' enthusiasm that the game will continue to prosper in this country.

As far as the Middlesex image is concerned, it has been tarnished in the last two days. Maybe the gentleman in the crowd should have sung, 'Sussex by the sea, where the ocean air is free, and the Middlesex team hasn't shown much to me.' Sad, but fairly accurate. This is the time when true character shines through – a testing time for my adopted club, the players, the coach and the supporters.

CHAPTER FOURTEEN
The End of the Season

Tuesday, 18 August – fry-ups and one-day cricket

Back from Sussex and back to the fresh and exciting London air. After a morning stroll with my family, the aroma of freshly brewed coffee and sizzling bacon on the West Hampstead café strip was too much of a temptation to disregard. Sitting at a round café table, plastic tablecloth and all, I ordered a traditional English breakfast advertised in the window as 'Special Treat – Full English Breakfast plus a free cappuccino, only £3.75'. How could my grumbling stomach, salivating taste buds and twitching nasal hairs resist that? Simple answer, they couldn't!

A full English breakfast, better known as a good old-fashioned fry-up, is a bloody marvellous affair, even for professional sportsmen keen on keeping some sort of respectable body shape during the summer.

The breakfast culture in London is something of an eye-opener. Pondering over my plate of fried delights – bacon, scrambled eggs, baked beans, sausage, mushrooms, tomato and toast – I became intrigued at the early-morning London thoroughfare. Drinking glorious cappuccino, I was in my element watching the world rush by – red London buses making their way through the traffic and narrow streets like tiger sharks making their way through schools of smaller fish; people in business attire smoking cigarettes, reading papers, sipping coffee or running frantically towards their bus stop or tube station; cyclists riding with gasmasks on their faces, obviously trying to keep their lungs from having to work overtime in the polluted city air; street tramps cracking their first can of cheap beer for the day.

Our waitress, wearing a 'Save the Animals' T-shirt and purple velvet skirt, and sporting dyed orange spiky hair, looked as though she had arrived at work straight from a nightclub. She didn't bother smiling much as she delivered cappuccinos and hot plates of English breakfasts to the various tables. Mind you, if I had my eyebrows, navel and lips pierced as many times as she had, I would also have trouble managing a cheerful morning smile for my customers.

You never feel as good after a fry-up as you do during it, but what the heck. In the environment I was in today, relaxing with my girls, it is worth putting up with the English breakfast aftertaste, which leaves your mouth feeling like you've just eaten a couple of spoonfuls of lard.

Away from the cricket, this summer has provided me with an opportunity to enjoy the cosmopolitan lifestyle of London. Worlds apart from my home-town, Perth, it is an excellent experience being able to walk down the road and taste the many facets of London. Ten minutes from the West End and five minutes from Lord's, we have been very fortunate for the last four months.

Off fry-ups and back to cricket. South Africa finished

off their long English summer with a win over England at Headingley in the final one-day international. They may not have qualified for Thursday's final at Lord's in the triangular series with Sri Lanka, but they did prove why they are arguably the most successful one-day team in international cricket. While the coloured clothes and white balls may have shocked England's cricket purists, I am sure it has given the English public a taste of what to expect come next summer's World Cup.

With the current World Cup champions, Sri Lanka, competing here against two top one-day teams in England and South Africa, the temptation to start predicting next year's champions is great. Nine months is a long time but the atmosphere in the UK is hotting up for what promises to be a crackerjack World Cup. This time next year, the new world champions will have raised the trophy at Lord's and donned the crown for the next four years. If England can host a World Cup that is as successful as the football campaign in France, we should be in for a sensational event.

I look forward to seeing that.

Thursday, 20 August – Sri Lanka, champions again!

It is no coincidence, or fluke, that Sri Lanka currently holds the title of the best one-day cricketing nation in the world. It is a remarkable achievement; it wasn't long ago that they were considered to be a third-world nation in terms of cricketing prowess. Beating England in the final of the Emirates tri-nation series is another feather in their coloured one-day playing caps. I wouldn't be surprised to see these caps growing wings from the volume of feathers being accumulated by these one-day wonders. Their game is a combination of excitingly aggressive batting, athletic fielding, enthusiastic appealing and steady, controlled bowling.

Heroes today included batsman Marvan Atapattu, a star in the making. He is technically supreme and while not as ruthless as Jayasuriya, Kaluwitharana or Aravinda de Silva, he still managed 130 not out in the allotted fifty overs – a magnificent innings which he controlled like a master conductor controls his orchestra. His partners chipped in with a couple of cameo knocks but he really stole the show on a perfect summer's day at beautiful Lord's. Head groundsman Mick Hunt will be as delighted with the state of the pitch he prepared as Atapattu was with batting on it.

Although the Sri Lankans' batting clinched the result, it was in fact a bowler who won the man-of-the-match award adjudged by David Gower. Muttiah Muralitharan, the controversial off-spinning genius, set up the game by taking five wickets.

England off-spinner Robert Croft was left scratching his head as he failed to extract half of the spin of Sri Lanka's star bowler. With two runs remaining, it looked like Crofty attempted to mimic the action of his Sri Lankan counterpart but in his effort he missed the turf strip. His wide only added to the perplexity of how one off-spinner can turn the ball so prodigiously in comparison with another.

Murali's international reputation is growing quickly. His statistics make remarkable reading and his influence on his team's rising fortunes is becoming quite pronounced. It is exciting to see spinners having such an incisive effect on the world stage. Warne, Saqlain, Mushtaq, Kumble and to a lesser extent Adams, Bevan and Symcox are all influential artists in the modern game.

Spin bowling, thought of as a dying art not so long ago, is rising like a determined phoenix thanks to the expertise of these masters. Muralitharan's dominance today has re-ignited the quest for England's best spinner. As I've mentioned before, in my eyes the best spinner in this country is my Middlesex team-mate Phil Tufnell. A proven match winner, it seems surprising that he isn't playing a more significant role for the England Test side. He has similar qualities of genius to the present masters. The only quality he lacks in comparison is the unwavering belief in himself that his contemporaries seem to possess. Cricket lovers would be in for a feast next week if both Murali and Tuffers were lining up for the one-off Test match at The Oval. In my view, it is a shame England's most talented spinner is unlikely to get the nod over Ian Salisbury or Robert Croft. I have a gut feeling Murali could run riot at The Oval. Having stood in the slips when Tuffers is bowling for the majority of the summer, I am confused at the English selectors' and the English press's desire to overlook the left-arm spinner. His bowling is special. There is no way he is not playing because he is not good enough.

He will be the first to admit that he is a different sort of character from the norm, but led strongly, I believe he could be one of the great spinners produced in England. He may not run the extra laps or push weights, but his heart is in the right place and I believe he does offer the team a lot on the field with his bowling. Continued ignoring of his talent will be a shame for English cricket, not only because he has the ability to win matches but he also entertains the cricket-loving English public who seem to be desperate for something to hold on to at the moment. It is heroes like Phil Tufnell who the crowds seem to relate to. This summer England has produced their heroes and the game will prosper because of it. The public can't get enough of a hero. Last summer it was Tuffers who won The Oval Test match for England. I remember it well because I was sitting in the Australian changing-room as Tuffers spun out my team-mates with aggressive and exciting bowling. By the look of this season's selection trend, we won't get the opportunity to see Tuffers in action next week against the Sri Lankans, a decision which can only be pleasing for the tourists.

Friday, 21 August – getting tired

Looking back over the last two months, I have noticed that there are a number of missed days in this diary account of an English summer. At first glance this may not seem a big deal, but to me it is a very significant comment on playing county cricket.

Keeping a diary requires discipline and application. While it is fun to do, it is at times hard work maintaining the enthusiasm to enter your thoughts every day. The missed entries are a clear indication to me of the frame of mind that I have slipped into as a result of playing cricket day in, day out. I have simply become very tired, both in mind and body.

It sounds crazy to say that I can judge the effect of a season of county cricket through my diminishing writing enthusiasm. In the past I have always cherished the chance to write about the day and I use it as a way to clear my thoughts and have a bit of fun. It has become a routine, just like practising cricket, that I have always enjoyed. Rarely have I considered it a chore to finish off my day with a few thoughts penned into my diary.

In the last few weeks, I don't seem to have had the energy to stick to this normal routine. Rather than writing, I have preferred to sit like a zombie in front of the television and watch *Ally McBeal* or *ER*, even the *Teletubbies*, with my feet up. It sounds slack, and I know it is probably more of an attitude thing than anything else, but it is just how I have been feeling.

There have been other, more worrying, telltale signs of this laziness resulting from tiredness. For one, my batting is suffering like my writing. I have been out leg before wicket more times in the last four months than I have in my entire career. This is a sure indication that my footwork has become a little lazier than I demand of myself and generally take for granted. While I am telling my feet to get moving, they seem to be hearing the request but, to my frustration, taking more time than usual to react. Apart from my feet, the season's statistics highlight that the second half of the summer hasn't been as abundant in terms of runs as was the first. This is undoubtedly a result of my lazier footwork; they go hand in hand, they always do.

These lazy habits and results, I can assure you, are not due to lack of trying on my part. I have tried to maintain my energy and form throughout the whole summer, but I have found that, no matter how hard I have tried to be consistent, it has been very hard work. There is a saying that 'the pain of discipline, is nothing like the pain of disappointment'. While I have lived by this adage for my whole career, I have found that as I have wearied from the constancy of county cricket, it has been difficult to maintain my discipline, no matter how hard I have tried. With an overload of the game, it is very difficult to stay in peak condition for the whole season.

It is very evident to me, as an overseas guest of county cricket, that this overload is bound to have a detrimental effect on the overall standard of the county game. First, take into account the extraordinary number of games played in a season – seventeen or eighteen first-class games, seventeen Sunday League games and two prestigious one-day competitions. Then consider that each day requires six and a half hours of play, plus an hour and a half's warm-up each morning. For good measure, include the travel to and from each venue, which can be up to an hour each way to the home ground. All this adds up to a timebomb for a great majority of the players, who also have to find time for their families and friends.

For many people these hours may seem like a normal set of circumstances for any working person. Perhaps that is right, but remember that cricket is a game that not only requires mental energy in concentration but also physical energy to be outside in all weathers for six and a half hours a day. It can be very demanding. A county cricketer is a bit like a car tyre with a slow leaking valve. At first the tyre is as hard as a rock and consequently performs at its optimum, allowing the car to run as smoothly as silk. Unfortunately, as you continue to use the car, the valve continues to leak and the tyre gets flatter and flatter with every use. Eventually it becomes so flat that the car can no longer function until you pump it up with more air. County cricketers come into a new season like the brand new car tyre – full of enthusiasm, full of energy and full of expectation for the new season. Renewed energy generally means optimum performance and optimum intensity. After a month or so, the slowly leaking valve starts to take its toll and the legs, back and brain start to slow down a little. As they become flatter, you get to the point where you're no longer performing at your peak, but rather just doing what you have to do to get to the next point of your destination. If the majority of county players start to feel this flatness, it is difficult, if not impossible, to maintain an intense, tough competition throughout.

People in England always ask me about the difference between cricket in Australia and cricket in England. The major difference in my eyes is the intensity of the game. In Australia, we play ten Shield games and five one-day games throughout the season. This in itself means that hunger for success is high. Every time I walk to the crease in Shield cricket, I know that I have to make the most of the opportunity. A failure or two will quickly have you sliding down the long waiting list for higher honours. There is no room for complacency in Shield cricket.

Fewer games means more time for preparation. Between games, players have time to work on their fitness levels, their technical needs and, most importantly, their frame of mind going into every game. Players have time to recover between fixtures, as well as analyse areas where they can make improvements. Hunger for success combined with well-prepared, generally well-disciplined players makes for tough competition closer to Test cricket than I would say county cricket has proved to be.

In contrast, the English system doesn't really allow for any recovery or preparation. The general attitude is that it is impossible to fit more work into an already hectic schedule. Quality is sacrificed for quantity in the English system. How is a player supposed to improve his technique and fitness level and remain fresh in mind and body when he is playing so regularly?

As with writing my diary, I have started telling myself that missing today is no big deal, I can always make up for it tomorrow. It is easy to keep putting it off, because putting it off means not having to work, and who wants to work if they don't really have to? That sounds terrible, doesn't it?

I get the feeling that English county cricket players can easily fall into this trap with their cricket. A batsman could easily start to think, 'Well, if I miss out on making runs today, that's no big deal because I can always make them tomorrow or the next day.' Let's face it, a county batsman is likely to have at least three innings a week so what's a few failures in a whole season? This is a lazy attitude that may spread like the plague through the county system.

While I would never dream of having that attitude in Sheffield Shield cricket, I can see how easily it can pervade the county game. I am not proud to admit it, in fact it makes me sad to say it, but there have been times when I have gone out to bat this summer and thought, 'Here we go again, another innings, maybe I can leave it until tomorrow.'

Ouch, it hurts to say that!

Books on motivation say it all comes down to attitude. They are right, and that is why I am writing now, but somehow and sometimes your brain has a knack of saying, 'Stick your attitude up your shirt, I want a rest.' How can you fight that?

Saturday, 22 August – bowled Phil Simmons

In a sad and disappointing conclusion to my first season with Middlesex we found ourselves at the wrong end of a very disciplined and 'together' Leicestershire team over the last couple of days. It will not surprise me in the slightest if I read from Pakistan that this team are the county champions for 1998.

Of all the teams that I have played against this summer, there is no doubt that Leicestershire are the closest and most disciplined team in the competition. They play it tough on the field and look to be enjoying each other's success at all times. It is difficult to find a chink in their armour in the way of talent and attitude towards the game. In my eyes, they will be at the top of the table come 13 September.

Apart from their star players like Darren Maddy, Vince Wells, Phil Simmons and Chris Lewis, the Leicester team are made up of a team of fighters who really play hard and work together on the field. One guy who really impressed me during this game was Iain Sutcliffe, who made one of the most ruthless centuries that I have ever seen on a cricket field. I never saw the great Graeme Pollock bat, but I imagine he would have regularly dispersed bowling attacks like Sutcliffe did to us yesterday. A strong left-hander with a bottom hand that is as dominant as Mike Tyson's left hook, he played an awesome innings of power and skill. It is players like him that make Leicestershire such a formidable team. While he is probably not considered one of their superstars of the team, he has just played an incredible match-winning innings that demoralised my team-mates and me.

From a personal point of view, it was a sickening sound that signalled the end of my season for Middlesex. After batting hard for a session, West Indian import Phil Simmons threaded an inswinger through my defence, dislodging my bails and at the same time dislodging any ambition I had of completing the summer with a big score. It would have been nice to finish with a century, but as so often happens, the game decided to send me off to Pakistan with some work to do in the Test series.

It would be remiss of me to play at Leicestershire and not mention the Barbadian cheer-leader who so loves his Leicester team. Like the Barmy Army, the entire Glamorgan crowd or the Sussex opera singer, it is people like this who truly add a special atmosphere to the game of cricket. He may give a lot of people a terrible headache, but I must admit, even though I would prefer it if he was supporting my team rather than theirs, he did provide me with mountains of humour over the last few days.

Even though my Australian selection means that I will miss the last three games for Middlesex, I would be lying if I didn't say today was tinged with a small thread of relief. Now that the season is over I can put my bats down for a week or so and recharge the batteries before heading off to Pakistan. It has been a disappointing season as far as our results have gone but I have had a great time, even if there have been a few minor frustrations along the way. Whether today was my last game of county cricket I don't know, but my gut feeling tells me that I will be back for another go at it next season.

Until then, there is a lot of cricket to be played. None more important than the Ashes series out in Australia, a series that I would love to be a part of if the opportunity presents itself. An Ashes series, as I have said so many times, is the ultimate cricket battle and, if the England team can play like Leicestershire play their cricket, we Aussies will be in for a tough series.

Thursday, 27 August – unemployment lines

'Get there early or you will be sorry,' was the advice from my experienced colleagues. 'If you are not there when the doors open, the queues are horrendous and you could be there all day.'

Aware that I was catching a plane back to Australia tonight, an 8.30 a.m. rendezvous in London City was hardly the ideal climax to what has been an exciting and eventful five months. Dragging myself out of bed was tough enough after last night's farewell 'swim-through' with my Middlesex team-mates, and my brain, as cloudy as an English winter day, was slowly starting to piece together the events of the previous hours. As my hired black cab pulled up outside the cast-iron gates of 1 Melton Street, it suddenly became clear what I was in for, for the remainder of this grey, bleak Thursday morning.

With a throbbing head, and a mouth that was as dry as a desert walker's foot, I paid my cab fare and trudged like a wounded soldier to the black, locked gates. After five months in the country I was finally securing that elusive National Insurance number that had eluded me, as a result of sheer laziness, for five chaotic months.

Lining up in the queue, the little devil on my shoulder

was coaxing, 'Forget it pal, you don't really need this number, you're wasting your time lining up all morning, get it next time you're in England, the tax people will never check it out anyway.'

The blue-eyed good angel on my other shoulder was fighting back, 'You know you have to get this number. Don't be an idiot, you have had five months, now stand your lazy arse in this line and get that number now or you will live to regret it.'

In the end the good angel shook me out of my self-induced stupor, and my resolve was strengthened to fight through this ordeal. Standing in the line, I could have easily been mistaken for someone in a police line-up down at Scotland Yard. I have had many memorable experiences but this one was a beauty. Here I was, unshaven, hung-over and dressed in a pair of jeans and a sweater, and blending in perfectly with the other men in the queue who were all looking desperate for the doors to open. The only difference between me and my new mates was that I didn't have a fag hanging out of my mouth, I didn't have any visible tattoos or earrings, and I was waiting for a number rather than my weekly benefit allowance.

Before the gates opened I enjoyed the opportunity of watching the London world that was racing by like a slick Mercedes Benz. Men in suits, tourists pulling suitcases, dreadlocked West Indians cruising along to the beat of their Walkmans and joggers out for their morning sweat-up.

Different people, varied cultures, different colours, different eyes, different agendas, all rushing by, in their own worlds, but with two obvious things in common. Firstly they all seemed to be in a hurry, and secondly they all had a sympathetic peek at the poor bastards standing in front of the unfriendly grey building awaiting their weekly dole money.

I am far from being a snob, but I must admit it was quite an uneasy feeling standing in this line-up. These boys all looked like they had done plenty of living in their times, and at a guess, I wouldn't imagine it would have taken much more than a curious glance to attract the wrath of their cumulated anger.

Inside, the atmosphere hadn't changed much from how it was out on the pavement. Like a scene from *The Full Monty*, the people inside were loud and abusive, and the security guards were on full alert for most of the time. When my number finally appeared on the TV monitor up above, I was greeted by an unfriendly, bored-looking lady who listened to my request before sliding a form under her thick glass window and told me to fill it out and wait to be called. I couldn't help but wonder how bored she was going to be acting come 4.30 in the afternoon, as she could only have clocked on half an hour before I had met her. That was her problem I guess!

After thirty minutes of answering all the questions and writing an essay that included everything from my mother's maiden name to my last five forms of employment, the social security officer plugged a few details into the computer before offering me a perplexed expression. 'Sorry to have wasted your time Mr Langer, but our records show that you already have a National Insurance number from when you were working up in Scotland in 1993.'

'Please tell me you are joking,' I pleaded with the officer. My head, already thumping like a solo saxophonist, instantly turned into the whole brass band. For five months I had been putting off this visit, and after ultimately succumbing to the pleas of the accountant, found myself in this hell-hole on my last day in London. Now I was being told that I shouldn't have wasted my time.

Rather than spending my concluding hours in the world's most exciting city looking at Big Ben, Hyde Park or Buckingham Palace, or even eating breakfast in Covent Garden, I was being mentally harassed by a bored social security woman on a cold, bleak morning. After being looked up and down by a dozen blokes who looked as though they had just escaped from the local jail, my nerves were in a tatter as I hailed yet another black cab. Soon I would be back in sleepy young Perth, eating off the bbq, drinking cold beer and remembering this character-building experience, not the first one for this English summer. I wouldn't have written the perfect script like this, but I suppose that is just part of the fun.

There was one big question occupying our minds as we boarded Cathay Pacific flight 254 to Hong Kong. Funnily enough, it was the same question that drove Sue and me crazy five months ago – would Jessica sleep at all on the way home? One whole day is a long time to chase a little girl around the cabin of a Jumbo jet at twenty thousand feet. Leg weary from five months of county cricket, the anticipation of twenty sleepless hours doing shuttle runs and rugby tackles up and down the aisles was enough to tempt a double dose of sleeping pills for both runners. Playing hide and seek in the cockpit of a Jumbo, or climbing over the pilot's knees to find my daughter at the controls of a man-made bird, are horrifying thoughts. Picturing her pushing colourful buttons while cheekily talking to the plastic autopilot about our preferred flight path had me calling for shots of tequila to wash down those sleeping pills.

Being the responsible father, the pills and tequila were a mythical escape from reality. Rather than checking the movie list in the entertainment guide, I pulled my running shoes from my hand luggage and prepared myself for the journey ahead. With Sue thirty weeks pregnant I knew the task at hand was likely to be a lonely one. A tired, waddling 'hippo', carrying our second addition to the family, is hardly your ideal wing-man for a task of this nature.

Wonderfully, and as before, London to Hong Kong was a breeze. The torturous 'no sleep' therapy we employed over our last twenty-four hours in London paid dividends. Jessica was so tired that she was asleep before the 'fasten seat belts' sign started flashing above our heads. For ten lovely hours I had a chance to sit back and reminisce about my first season as an overseas county pro.

Reflecting on five months of county cricket, the happy memories outweigh the negative ones – a feast of batting, ample time to improve my cricket, fantastic cricket grounds (including the obvious one), good people and an exciting lifestyle in London. It is something of a dream being able to earn a good living playing cricket day in, day out. Although the mind and body are a little worse for wear, I couldn't think of a better lifestyle for a cricket fanatic like myself.

Life at Lord's is marvellous. I have described the joy of playing on the hallowed turf several times in these pages, and the ups and downs of returning through the Long Room, and how the thrill was like a spirit that embraced me every time I entered the ground. It was with me everywhere. From eating my breakfast on the players' balcony to fielding in the slips, this spirit, encompassed by the terracotta-coloured grandpa pavilion, acted as a loyal ally while I wore the royal blue Middlesex cap. It was quite a privilege being allowed to walk through the Long Room in my tracksuit and sneakers rather than the mandatory jacket and tie. To ensure that I never abused this privilege, or for a second took the place for granted, I was regularly pulled back into reality by the paintings of Bradman, Miller and Compton staring down at me from the walls. Their stern looks almost dared me to step one foot out of line and face the wrath of their infinite existence.

In the wash up, Middlesex have had a disappointing season. There are many reasons for this but none simpler than the fact that we lacked on-field experience all season. With the absence of England stars Angus Fraser and Ramps for the majority of the summer, we were regularly fielding a fairly inexperienced first eleven. Obviously Gatt, Tuffers, Browny and, to a lesser extent, Paul Weekes offered some experience, but the make-up of the team left us undermanned and less competitive than we would have liked.

One of the big problems with county cricket is that the system below first-class cricket doesn't seem to offer tough enough schooling for players to arrive on the scene well prepared for the higher level. For example, a player like Tim Bloomfield, opening the bowling for Middlesex at Lord's, is expected to bowl out players like Brian Lara, Carl Hooper, Graeme Hick and Chris Adams. Only twelve months ago he was playing village/club cricket in one of the local London leagues. Having seen the general standard and intensity of English club cricket, I would say it is hardly the ideal stepping-stone for intimidating world-class players.

Club cricket may teach young players how to run in and bowl to club batsmen, and how to smash amateur bowlers around the park, but it is rarely going to teach them the importance of the key elements of successful first-class cricket. In Australia, players generally come into first-class cricket with a clear understanding of what it will take to be successful. Important issues like attaining and maintaining a high level of fitness, an understanding of how to bowl a consistent line and length, and reasonable experience of how to handle the pressure of four-day cricket, have all been addressed.

Sure, Australian youngsters need to learn, make mistakes and hopefully improve like their English contemporaries, but at least they generally have a solid foundation to start with. In English league cricket, a number of these young players may learn more about enjoying a pint of beer and having a few laughs on the cricket field than stretching their muscles, visualising how to attack the opposition or batting as if their life depended upon it. Don't get me wrong, English club cricket is a brilliant way to enjoy our great game, but I don't believe it is the best way for young players to develop into serious contenders for first-class cricket.

As an overseas player, I found this to be frustrating. First-class cricket is the level below Test cricket, and yet at times it felt like county cricket was acting as a finishing school for first-class cricket. I am told that the second-eleven competition has lowered in standard over the last few years, leaving the youngsters very raw when it comes to the rounded package of a first-class player.

In my eyes, players should have to fight to make the first-class ranks. On reaching this level, they should listen, learn and constantly work to improve their game by using their own experience, and the experience and wisdom of their more senior team-mates. I haven't seen enough of this system this summer.

The Australian Cricket Academy is one example of proven acceleration from junior or club cricket to first-class level. An England-based academy could work as long as the right players were chosen and the right programmes and coaches were employed. Rod Marsh is the current head coach of the Academy and every young player knows that he daren't break any rules or he will find himself face to face in Rodney's office. Knowing the tough demeanour of Australia's former international wicketkeeper, this is a frightening prospect for any aspiring young cricketer hoping to graduate from the esteemed Cricket Academy.

In a ten-month programme, the top eighteen young players from all around Australia are chosen and offered an outstanding opportunity to improve all their cricketing skills. This development process includes technical improvement, sports psychology, physical fitness programmes and understanding and respect for the history of the game. By studying all these facets, a young player is given the opportunity to lay the foundations of becoming a top-class competitor in first-class cricket. Those players who don't go to the Academy learn the game in grade cricket, where its intensity and competitiveness act as fairly strong stepping-stones into Sheffield Shield cricket.

It seems the English authorities need to find a way of producing a system where the younger players enter the first-class system better equipped for the task at hand. From the many changing-room, committee-room, and bar-room discussions that I have had over the last five months, it is obvious that many people have opinions on how this can be achieved. I only hope, for the sake of county cricket, that all the discussion is channelled effectively, and quickly, to find the best answer.

The young players must be encouraged and nurtured in an environment where striving for excellence is the main priority. There is no doubting that there are a number of talented young players like Tim Bloomfield out there playing cricket around the country. While the counties are striving hard to identify this talent, I think the next step should be a strong focus on providing a clear path for the best young players, encouraging them to aim to play Test cricket. If playing Test cricket becomes so strong an ambition that every young player desperately seeks the honour, the standard of county cricket will look after itself.

So much of the discussion around county cricket centres on the sheer quantity of cricket played. As an outsider used to playing a third of the amount of cricket in an Australian summer, I have to admit I can see how hard it is for the county players to maintain a killer instinct. Unfortunately, the county game potentially promotes a system under which its players view the game as a job rather than a sport, or even an art. From my experience, it takes a massive effort to retain the same hunger and motivation to produce consistently inspired performances every day. No matter how hard I tried, I will be the first to admit it became increasingly difficult to stay pumped up for every game.

It is difficult to expect the fast bowlers to run in

vigorously every day and perform such an unnatural act day in, day out. Physically it takes its toll and mentally the doubts and barriers in a bowler's mind increasingly hinder consistent performance. As a batsman, I knew that by working through the tough periods the pickings would be very fruitful, not because of the lack of talented bowlers trying to get me out, but rather as a result of the dwindling physical and mental stamina of the majority of the circuit bowlers. As the season wore on, batting became more of a battle of the minds between the leg-sore bowlers and the greedy, run-hungry batsmen like myself.

The deteriorating hunger for consistent success is not the fault of the individuals; at the end of the day, I am sure everyone is out there busting their guts to win and play well. Because of the number of match days, I feel many of the players find it difficult to put in the extra work to improve their games. Often the encouragement for a greater work ethic is met with an enthusiastic response, rarely backed up with much action. It is very easy to talk a good game. Stepping out of the comfort zone and actually pro-actively attempting to become a better player is another thing. Often the mind may be willing but the body is pleading for a rest; alternatively, the body may be fit and keen but the mind is longing for a break between concentration bursts.

Much of our season at Middlesex was dogged by media reports of internal problems within the ranks. John Buchanan, employed by the club to introduce a new style of coaching, was reportedly frustrated by the culture of county cricket. Change takes time and, considering the success of Middlesex under Mike Gatting and coach Don Bennett, the changing face of the club hierarchy was sure to meet certain barriers. I hope that Buck returns to London next year to build on the foundations of élite preparation he introduced to the playing staff this season. I am a big fan of his and I feel his style of coaching will pay dividends if the team continues to grasp his method with enthusiasm. With the young, inexperienced players coming through, I believe his expertise can only help accelerate their development.

With my stay cut three games short by selection for the Aussie Test team to Pakistan, I feel disappointed not to finish off the season with my new team-mates. It will be difficult watching the results on the Internet, wondering if I could be making a difference by being there with them. I am no martyr, but I will say that I would exchange half the runs I scored this summer for more team success at Middlesex. There is no success like team success and I dearly wish I was sitting on this flight enjoying my daughter's long sleep while remembering a B&H or NatWest Cup victory, or even a few more outright championship victories. Middlesex are in a rebuilding stage and I am sure, with everyone's commitment, the outstanding tradition of success enjoyed by this fine club will soon be revisited. I look forward to being a part of the exciting challenge of pushing MCCC back to the forefront of county cricket next season.

Oh no, time for a stretch, cuddle, something to eat and a warm bottle of milk. My video monitor tells me there are fifty-four minutes to touchdown at the new Hong Kong airport and I can see Jess sitting up wiping her eyes and looking around like a newly hatched chick. We nearly made it the whole way. My daughter is a bloody champion, if I say so myself.

* * *

As for me, I am thrilled to have had the opportunity to play county cricket. Playing against varied attacks in varying conditions is sure to have helped my personal development as a player. I know it is one of the pet hates of many English cricket supporters, but I hope the experience of county cricket will help me compete more fiercely against the old enemy this Australian summer.

This Ashes series promises to be one of the great ones. If England can continue to play with the same intensity and passion they showed this summer, they will be very, very competitive. Alec Stewart knows Australia and, more appropriately, Australians. He has spent many years here in his quest for continued improvement and I am sure his expertise in reading the Aussie style of play will be a telling factor.

The England team needs to win this Ashes series. Their players are all in the prime of their careers. The whole of the top order is talented and experienced, while the fast bowling department looks confident and capable of destructive feats. Their defeat against Sri Lanka should be a minor hiccup and if they take all of the positives out of this summer, we will be in for a street fight of the highest order.

The convicts, as we are so affectionately known by many paying English spectators, will be primed up and ready to go. There is nothing like an Ashes series, nothing like a battle between the poms and the convicts. This one could be a fight to the finish. If I were a betting man, I would definitely have five dollars on the good guys . . .

Leaving out Phil Tufnell could be a telling selection. Time will tell.

Bon voyage to England. Thanks for a great experience.

EPILOGUE

September 1998–April 1999 – the winter

It was hard watching the Internet from Perth and Pakistan, and seeing the flagging fortunes of my newly adopted team. Having missed the last three games of the season because of my selection in the Aussie touring team to Pakistan, I could only cringe at the disappointing end to the season. Although we were in the top half of the table in the Sunday League for most of the summer, losses in the last three games meant that we will compete in the second division of that competition next summer. In the championship we finished well down in the table, rounding off a very unsatisfactory season. What started out so promisingly ended so disappointingly. A new coach in April looked to be igniting real direction and enthusiasm into Middlesex County Cricket Club, but, as has been well documented, the initial fire eventually faded into a dull flicker.

John Buchanan won't be back next season. In a word this is also disappointing, but not unexpected. Knowing Buck, this season won't be his last in county cricket. Having talked to him over the Australian summer, I get the feeling he learned a lot about the county season and he would like to have another go at it if the opportunity presents itself. County cricket is so different from Sheffield Shield cricket in Australia that adjustments must be made, and I am sure that would be the biggest lesson learnt by Shield cricket's most innovative, and arguably successful, coach over the last five years. At home there is ample time between every game for the coach to prepare his players physically, mentally and technically for the fixture ahead. Players have time to work on areas of their game which may need some quality time and practice, and the coach has the time and facilities to put his skills to work. In contrast, the county coach has less time between fixtures to demand the same effort from his players. I believe this is one of the reasons why a lot of county cricket players have basic technical problems, which lead to mediocre performances. Time is a key factor. We seem to have relatively more time to get things right, if a player wants to of course, whereas the county players are either playing a game, travelling up and down the motorway or trying to rest and recharge their physical batteries. It is something of a contradiction that county players play so much cricket, and yet they don't have the extra time to put into their games.

There has been so much talk about Middlesex's disappointing season. Middlesex is a club that is steeped in tradition. It has had so much success over the years that a season like this is a terrible shock to the system, almost an embarrassment for the club's history. The Middlesex spirits, so used to winning and enjoying success, can almost be felt frowning upon the class of 1998. Not unlike West Indian cricket after their tour of South Africa and the first Test against the Aussies, Middlesex need to rebuild and look positively towards the future.

The West Indies have been the dominant force in international cricket for decades and yet they returned home from South Africa with their supporters crying out for answers. The Caribbean people love their cricket more than any people I have ever seen. For as long as I know, they have been worshipping their cricket successes like a religion. When things weren't going as smoothly as they had for so many years, the West Indies were almost in a state of mourning. While Middlesex doesn't need to mourn, we do need to find the answers that will make us more competitive on the field next season. It is easy to point the finger at John Buchanan, the captain Mark Ramprakash, communication breakdowns between the administration and the captain and the coach, or a misunderstanding over who was meant to be running the show. For me, I am not sure whether these are reasons or just excuses.

If you were to ask me, it is the playing staff who have to take responsibility for our mediocre season. In the end, if a cricket team doesn't make enough runs, take enough wickets or catch all their catches, then they can't expect to enjoy the sweet taste of success. We didn't do enough of all these things for a great part of the season, hence our standings at the end of September. Cricket is a basic game made so complicated. Team spirit, fitness, discipline, patience, determination, pride in performance and so on are crucial components that enhance the prospect of success, but basically cricket is about making more runs than the opposition and taking twenty opposition wickets for a victory. Unfortunately we didn't do this during the summer of 1998, and our performances suffered because of it.

It seemed a natural progression that Mike Gatting

should be appointed coach for the 1999 season. From a personal point of view I am disappointed that he has retired from playing, as I would have loved to see him reach the target of one hundred first-class centuries. The most important thing is that he obviously feels the time is right to finish playing. He apparently wants to turn his concentration and focus onto coaching his beloved Middlesex club back into being a force, once again, in county cricket, and I can respect how he feels. I must admit, though, I wouldn't have minded sharing a few more moments with him out in the middle, as he was a fantastic guy to play with this summer. I had a brilliant time on the field with him. No doubt we will have as much fun as a player and coach combination next summer. If he coaches with the same focus and enthusiasm that he has played with throughout his career then he should be successful. Gatt is a part of the furniture at Middlesex and I am sure that his experiences in the fruitful years will be all the incentive he needs to put our train back on track.

The Ashes battle was a tough one, perhaps tougher than the three-one scoreline suggested. I knew we were going to be in for a Holyfield/Tyson-style scrap after the first game of the summer. Having returned home from Pakistan I was chosen to captain my home state of Western Australia against England at the WACA. After winning the toss and batting I found myself out in the middle facing Gough, Cork and Angus Fraser. If I thought I was in for a friendly walk in the park against the Englishmen then I was in for a rude awakening. Before long I was having a very colourful verbal punch-up with Darren Gough. If you thought Aussies were meant to be bad 'sledgers' then you should have heard Goughy going off his head. It was on for young and old as they say.

After ducking and weaving his bouncers on a very fast and bouncy pitch and taking his stares and insults I told him that he had an ego the size of the Lillee/Marsh stand. Goughy didn't take too kindly to this, so he told me that I couldn't play Test cricket, I was an average player and that I'd better watch out for the likes of Blewett, Elliott and Hayden because they were far better players than I would ever be. He then went on to say things that I would never say in front of my mum or grandmother. It was great stuff, just what it is all about. Luckily I scored a few runs, but he eventually had me caught and bowled. Oh, that hurt!

At the end of the game, Goughy smiled at me and told me he was looking forward to the Test series. I also smiled and told him that I was equally keen to get the big games under way. As it turned out we both had reasonable Test series. He was a little unlucky not to have had better figures mainly due to the dreaded dropped catches, but even so we had a number of tough encounters against each other. In the end I think the score between Gough and Langer was pretty even, as he dismissed me a couple of times, and I scored a few runs off his bowling.

Before he left our Sydney Cricket Ground changing-room on the final afternoon when the series was over, Goughy patted me on the shoulder, smiled his big smile and said, 'Well done mate, good series, respect mate, respect. I gave you a hard time at the WACA at the start of the tour, but you have done well and I have enjoyed the battle.' For me it was nice to hear this from one of the best competitors in international cricket. Having come back from Pakistan with my first Test century I was very keen to cement my position as Australia's number three batsman. During the season there was always pressure on me to achieve this and until the third Test in Adelaide I never felt truly comfortable. A compliment from Goughy after five Ashes Test matches was a small indication that I am on my way to regularly batting at number three for Australia.

Looking back at the series I think there were a few differences between the two teams. Both sides were talented on paper, both were fit and physically ready and both seemed to have a strong team spirit. To me the distinguishing feature of the result lay basically in the execution of a game plan. Our batsmen tended to go on and score big hundreds individually and as partnerships. Generally we capitalised on mistakes in the field and looked to bat hard in the toughest times. In the field we dropped fewer catches and our bowlers rarely gave the English batsmen an easy time in the middle. These points may sound simple and general, but it is usually the simple things, the basics, that make all the difference.

From my experience last summer in county cricket, I am not surprised at this difference in execution of the basics. Throughout the summer I didn't see a lot of players in the county system dominating with the bat and scoring big hundreds with any regularity. John Crawley and Graeme Hick aside, no English player scored consistent hundreds or consistent runs for the season. The thing is, if players don't learn to score big runs at county level then how can they be expected to step up and score hundreds in Test cricket? The old argument is that county cricket is weak, so it doesn't matter whether a player scores runs in county cricket. In my opinion this is absolute rubbish. Batting is about learning how to survive, learning how to make runs, and you cannot do this unless you are out in the middle doing just that, no matter what the opposition is like. Scoring runs is a habit and you can't nurture this habit unless you are doing it regularly.

Sure, further improvement will come by playing tougher opposition, but while the county system remains as it is now, everyone from playing staff to administration needs to work towards lifting the level of expectation from mediocrity to excellence. If nothing else, this will at least start the ball rolling towards a tougher, more competitive environment. As it is, many players in county cricket get away with mediocre performances and as a result I feel the Test team is suffering. If players in county cricket are rarely placed under constant pressure to perform, then they will never learn to make big runs when it counts, when the pressure is really on like it is in Test cricket. Maybe the numbers on each staff could be cut back so that there is pressure to perform. Only then will mediocre grounding be eliminated. A player could not then afford to get lazy and accept mediocrity. If he did then he might find himself working on a construction site or in an office like the large majority of the population.

Until this year an Australian first-class player didn't earn one cent unless he was playing in the first eleven. With this system it soon becomes apparent which players have the talent and desire to make it at first-class level. No player can afford to underachieve because there is always someone waiting to take his place. I think this is why Australian cricket is so strong. Because of the intense competition for places, players have to improve, they have to perform, they have to live by the law of 'the survival of the fittest'. Because we are brought up in this environment we learn how to play under pressure so that when we step up into Test cricket the chances of survival and consistent performance are enhanced.

As a batsman in this series, I would have to say that the English bowlers didn't maintain the pressure for as long as our bowlers probably did. England has some very talented bowlers. Gough, Mullally, Headley, Fraser and co. are top-line bowlers who can trouble any batsman in the world. The only difference is that they don't seem to maintain a disciplined line and length for as long as they could. You feel that if you can get through the tough times then the intensity will quickly drop off. I don't blame the bowlers for this; again I think that is how they are brought up in the county system. When you bowl nearly every day, it is physically and mentally impossible to keep up the same intensity all the time. Because they learn to play like this, it is hard to change, even if you are playing a Test match. Even with Darren Gough, who is a fantastic competitor and outstanding bowler, there were times when you felt that he wasn't all over you like one of those cheap synthetic suits you buy at London markets. In contrast you rarely see Glenn McGrath, Shane Warne or Damien Fleming give the batsmen a loose ball, or Ambrose, Walsh, Akram or Donald give you a slight breather for an over or two in a Test match.

During the summer I commented on the monumental job Alec Stewart was expected to do for his country, captaining, batting and wicketkeeping. I know Alec pretty well as he has spent a great deal of time in Perth. In the changing-rooms after the Boxing Day Test I asked him politely, but with a hint of sarcasm, whether or not he had woken up to one simple fact yet. He looked quizzical before I told him that if he ever played another Test match for England without opening the batting then he must have rocks in his head. Alec is also one of the game's toughest competitors who also happens to be one of the best opening batsmen in the world. After his brilliant century in Melbourne, when he opened the batting, he would be crazy not to continue in this role. Doing all three jobs is a massive responsibility at the Test level; if I was him I would concentrate on opening the batting and captaining the side.

But, then again, who am I to say?

I would be lying if I didn't say that it was a tremendous feeling beating the poms in an Ashes series. Having to listen to the Barmy Army for six hours a day, for twenty-one days, gave us that extra incentive to win the tough sessions. There is no denying that you have to admire the Barmy Army's tenacity and dedication to their beloved team. I just wish that for one day they were Mark Taylor's Aussie Barmy Army, on our side rather than theirs. Unfortunately that will never happen, so we will just have to keep smiling and use them to our advantage in the future.

For me, I will be back, and am looking forward to the challenge of another season of county cricket. Middlesex look to be very progressive in their vision for cricket in the next millennium and I am aspiring towards being a part of their future. Having just lived out an ambition of playing a full Ashes series I look forward to renewing my battle with Darren Gough, Alan Mullally, Dean Headley, Nasser Hussain, Alec Stewart and the rest of the Englishmen, as well as teaming up with Ramps and Gus Fraser for another season.

It will be nice to walk onto the cricket field with Ramps again this summer. He was something of a nemesis for me throughout the Ashes series. If he wasn't taking spectacular catches to dismiss me when I was batting, he was getting me out with his part-time off-spinners or smashing pull shots into my legs while I fielded at short leg. He is a very determined fighter who I will enjoy working with in 1999. I am also looking forward to living back in London for another six months. Horror parking, hectic motorways, traffic jams, public hospitals, warm beer and expensive steak aside, I love London and in fact all of England as a whole. We have some fantastic friends in the Motherland and we look forward to making lots more pommy friends over the years.

Although there has been a lot of talk about changing county cricket, I feel people should never lose sight of the fact that English cricket is a wonderful institution. Yes, certain areas of the county game need refining, but at the end of the day people should never forget that the game offers a great deal to many, many people. From spectators, to supporters, to administrators, to players, to umpires, the game is still alive and well. There is much that is great about English cricket.

Let's face it, if it was perfect what would people have to talk about?

International cricket today is a very hectic schedule which takes up twelve months of the calendar year. For this boy from the Outback I couldn't dream of a better way to live my life and I cherish my time living in the outfields of England, the West Indies, Australia, Pakistan, or wherever my cricket bat may take me.

From Outback to Outfield.

More terrific sports writing from Headline

A Lot of Hard Yakka

Triumph and torment: a county cricketer's life

SIMON HUGHES

William Hill Sports Book of the Year

'Terrific' Harold Pinter

'As life-lived-through-sport, it is pure Hornby, while the sex-and-booze boys-on-tour elements tap into the *Loaded* market' Simon Wilde, *The Times*

'A very funny, often outrageous book' Ian Wooldridge, *Daily Mail*

'Sharp and funny . . . lays bare the real truth of the athlete: a dark life of angst and self-doubt lit by sudden piercing shafts of transcendent adequacy' Simon Barnes

'You won't read a better inside story of cricket and the men who play it for a living' Michael Parkinson

Beneath professional cricket's monotonous, poorly paid routine is a soap opera of diverse characters living together through their ups and downs. In a way no other book has done, *A Lot of Hard Yakka* takes you behind the scenes for a real insight into how the household names of the last two decades – Botham, Brearley, Gatting, Gooch – survive their turbulent ride. Simon Hughes clung aboard for fifteen years, surfing the peaks and troughs with the great, the good and the ghastly. His series of warts-and-all vignettes is the most revealing, entertaining and honest book about cricket ever published.

NON-FICTION / SPORT 0 7472 5516 4